THE WISDOM OF THE DESERT FATHERS

September 1990

John,

May you find
this book of
spiritual flowers
a source of joy &
restful recovery,

In Christ,

Brigida Cobb

A

Also by BENEDICTA WARD SLG

The Prayers and Meditations of Saint Anselm with the Proslogion
(Penguin Classics)
Anselm of Canterbury: A Monastic Scholar (SLG Press)
The Sayings of the Desert Fathers (Mowbrays)
The Lives of the Desert Fathers (Mowbrays)
Miracles and the Medieval Mind (Scolar Press)

THE WISDOM OF THE DESERT FATHERS

SYSTEMATIC SAYINGS

from the

ANONYMOUS SERIES

OF THE *APOPHTHEGMATA PATRUM*

Translated with an Introduction by
SISTER BENEDICTA WARD SLG
Foreword by
Metropolitan Anthony Bloom

SLG PRESS
Convent of the Incarnation
Fairacres   Oxford

New Edition 1986

ISBN 0 7283 0109 1
ISSN 0307-1405

ACKNOWLEDGEMENTS

The cover picture, St Jerome Reading in a Landscape, *a drawing by Rembrandt, is reproduced here by kind permission of the Director of the Kunsthalle, Hamburg.*

The Portrait of a Young Boy *on p. viii is reproduced here by courtesy of the Trustees of the British Museum.*

CONTENTS

FOREWORD

THE TRADITION of 'the Desert Fathers is central to Christianity and I am certain that the Sayings of the Fathers have a great deal to teach us today. They should not be read, however, in an unrealistic or romantic way. It is not the desert that makes a desert father any more than it is the lion that makes the martyr. The desert is present everywhere and the spirituality of the desert can be found everywhere. We often make a mistake about the desert fathers and look for the wrong thing in their lives. It can sound as if the monks went around the desert trying to outdo each other in asceticism while their disciples sat around scoring points. But this is not at all what it is about. Man can derive his life either from God or from the earth and one way in which the lives of the desert saints can convey to us how much they depended on God, is to show us how little they depended upon earth. Ultimately, for the desert fathers it is not a question of more and more asceticism for its own sake, but they become more and more free because of it, until in the end they are like the mystical tree of China which grows with its roots heavenwards, uprooted here, rooted there.

The true spirituality of the desert is radical. Its essence is absolute simplicity, that consciousness that a man stands before God, establishing a relatedness between the two which is all-embracing because there is nothing that is outside it. Then the whole desert blossoms with meaning, the whole cosmos is guarded round. This is the essence of these Sayings and this belongs to our times as much as to any. We must go to this single, basic, radical Christianity, which does not mean trying to copy what they did, but we must learn from them a crystal-like simplicity.

This translation of the Sayings of the Fathers offers a way into this dimension of life and of prayer.

+ ANTHONY BLOOM
Metropolitan of Sourozh

Portrait of a Young Boy

This painting has been executed in encaustic on a thin panel, still attached to the mummy. From Hawara, Egypt, second century AD.

INTRODUCTION

THE WISDOM OF THE DESERT FATHERS is a collection of material which forms part of the records of the origins of Christian monasticism. In the fourth century, Egypt, Syria and Palestine were the scenes of intensive asceticism virtually new in the Christian world. Every form of monastic life was tried, and reshaped according to the content of the Gospel. By AD 400 Egypt could be described as a land of hermits, a source of exasperation to the civil authorities, who preferred men to work, fight and pay taxes and a focus for enthusiastic, if at times misguided, admiration from Christians in the East and soon also in the West.

Three main types of monastic experiment in Egypt correspond roughly to three geographical locations. In Lower Egypt St Antony the Great lived as a hermit and drew disciples to him who followed his way of life in solitude. In Upper Egypt there evolved a different form of the radical break with society in groups who lived in large communities under the inspiration of Saint Pachomius. Between these two extremes of eremitic and cenobitic life there emerged the *lavra* or *skete*, small groups living near a spiritual father and probably near a church where they could meet at weekends for the liturgy; these groups were found most of all in Nitria (see map). In Palestine, Syria and Asia Minor there were also Christians who were involved in the ascetic life in its monastic forms, and some stories and sayings from these areas are occasionally found among the Egyptian sources, but it was Egypt that most attracted attention and produced written records which were to influence the monastic world continually. Reforms of monastic life, whether in Italy and France in the twelfth century or in America in the twentieth, look at these records for inspiration.

There are the accounts of the lives of famous ascetics, such as St Antony and St Pachomius; there are some letters and longer exhortations (cf. *The Letters of St Antony the Great* and *The Letters of Ammonas*, SLG Press); there are travellers' accounts of visits to the desert, such as the *Lausiac History* of Palladius, or the adventures of seven monks from Palestine who wrote about their visit in the *Historia Monachorum in Aegypto* (*The Lives of the Desert Fathers*, Mowbrays, 1981). But most illuminating of all are the collections of sayings, anecdotes and short stories called the *Apophthegmata Patrum* of which the present collection forms part.

It seems that the sayings of some of the hermits were remembered and passed on from one monk to another and were eventually written down, usually in Greek. They were collected together in two main ways: either arranged alphabetically under the names of well-known monks (the Alphabetical Collection, translated by the present writer and published under the title *The Sayings of the Desert Fathers*, Mowbrays, 1983) or as sayings and stories related to some of the main themes of interest in the desert—the Systematic Series. Groups of monks would preserve the sayings of their founder or spiritual father and this nucleus would be rearranged and enlarged as time went on, in either of these two forms. They were eventually translated into other languages and in the West became widely known especially in monastic circles in the Latin version, the *Vitae Patrum*.

Written texts always add a certain sophistication to material and these collections of sayings and stories are no exception. However, it is possible to discover in these texts more of the simple and straight-forward wisom of the desert than elsewhere. The sayings do not provide a full or coherent programme of monastic life; they present, rather, instances of the action of God as experienced by the practical and for the most part unlettered men who were prepared to stake their lives on the fact of the resurrection of Jesus Christ. They are not photographs, giving exact details about people and places, nor are they icons, presenting eternal verity through the veil of appearances; they are more like the painting on wax to be found in the Coptic Gallery of the British Museum. These are vivid and colourful pictures of the Egyptian dead from second to fourth-century Egypt and it is possible to look with their eyes into the unexplored country on the other side of death, and to glimpse their experience of standing in the antechamber of the world to come.

The Systematic Series of sayings which is translated here consists in short sayings which were arranged in the fifth century in sections under subject heading. The sections reflect those themes of monastic life which were most clearly, though not exclusively, of interest to monks.

The themes found here, such as 'discernment', 'silence', 'obedience' and 'humility' are dealt with more extensively in other early writers, such as John Cassian, Evagrius and St John Climacus. The stories, similarly, which have been translated in the companion volume to this book, *The World of the Desert Fathers,* are mainly but not exclusively about monks, and can be supplemented from other accounts of the desert already mentioned. Both sayings and stories were compiled with a monastic audience in mind, but the ideas behind them are not of interest to monks alone. The monks did not, of course, claim to be the only Christians, nor the best Christians. They were simply men following out the Christian vocation in a particular way, which seemed to those observing them dramatic and intense. The virtues and obligations inherent in the Gospel for all are presented in the literature of the desert in stark and vivid colours, like a poster in their clarity. The monks saw themselves not as better than others but as more needy, more sinful and therefore more ready to receive the mercy of God; if they could be saved, they thought, there was then hope for everyone. As a later writer put it:

> God is the life of all free beings. He is the salvation of believers and unbelievers, of the just or the unjust . . . of monks or those living in the world, of the educated or the illiterate, of the healthy or the sick, of the young or the very old. He is like the outpouring of light, the glimpse of the sun, or the changes of the weather which are the same for everyone without exception.

(St John Climacus, *The Ladder of Divine Ascent,* trans. C. Luibheid and N. Russell, Classics of Western Spirituality, Paulist Press 1983, p.74.)

The Systematic Series is designed to illustrate above all the virtues of charity and humility. The texts are not mystical but ascetic, concerned with action—behaviour—not mystical experience. Indeed, several texts illustrate a suspicion of revelation and vision which is very striking. For instance, in the section dealing with humility, there is a story about a brother who was assured that he was in the presence of the Archangel Gabriel. His response was to say, 'See if it is not someone else to whom you have been sent; as for me, I am not worthy of it' (178. p.50). Other stories in the same section relate how monks refused to believe they were in the presence of Christ, with similar phrases, 'I am not worthy' or 'I do not want to see Christ here below'. Claims to direct and private revelation were held suspect, but genuine humility had its reward: a monk who wanted to know how a particular part of the Scriptures should be under-stood received no reply when he prayed for God to reveal this to him, but the moment he decided to go and ask his brother about it, an angel of the Lord appeared and said, 'When you humbled yourself by going to see your brother, then I was sent to tell you the meaning of this saying.' (182, p.50.)

This solid realism of charity and humility is not a solemn and depressing thing. These sayings have in them a certain bite of humour, as can be seen in the reply already quoted of a monk to the Archangel. The story of two monks who thought they ought to have a quarrel, 'in order to be like other men', and could not manage it, was surely told in Scetis with a certain humour:

Two old men had lived together for many years and had never fought with one another. The first said to the other, 'Let us also have a fight like other men do.' The other replied, 'I do not know how to fight.' The first said to him, 'Look, I will put a brick between us, and will say it is mine, and you say, "No, it is mine", and so the fight will begin.' So they put a brick between them and the first said, 'This brick is mine', and the other said, 'No, it is mine', and the first responded, 'If it is yours, take it and go'—so they gave it up without being able to find an occasion for argument.   (221, p.60.)

There is a certain joy inherent in the picture of the early days of desert monasticism. One saying describes the monks as building a cell, presumably for newcomers, in terms of unity and enthusiasm: 'They went joyfully to build the foundations and did not stop till it was finished' (230, p.62). There is even here a story of a monk who provided meals for brothers who were making journeys into the town, and gave them refreshment 'with all his heart'. The priority of charity is not forced but natural. 'A brother went to see an anchorite and as he was leaving he said to him, "Forgive me, abba, for having taken you away from your rule." But the other answered him, "My rule is to refresh you and send you away in peace."' (151, p.42.)

The charity of the monks is not to be confused with social service. Again and again in this collection it is made clear that the work of the monk is not to intervene in the lives of others but to labour to be transformed into Christ so that his presence may be known in the world. In this collection, it is the 'pagans', not the monks, who go into Ostrakina and offer alms, bread, clothing, to those in need; and the poor of the city refuse this help in the same phrases as those used by the monks, 'I have God who cares for me, and would you really deprive me of that?' (131, pp. 38–39). The second saying in this collection expresses the approach of the monks to the commandments of love very delicately. Three friends wished to serve God with all their hearts but they chose to do so in different ways. One of them chose to be a peace-maker among men, another chose to visit the sick, and both found they could be of very little help in their spheres of social action. Discouraged, they went to visit the third, who had chosen to live alone and in stillness; he used an acted parable to demonstrate the work of the monk, with the suggestion that the basic requirement for all Christians is to become still and allow God to act through them:

> After a short silence, he poured some water into a bowl and said to them, 'Look at the water', and it was disturbed. After a little while he said to them again, 'Look how still the water is now', and as they looked into the water, they saw their own faces reflected in it as in a mirror. Then he said to them, 'It is the same for those who live among men; disturbances prevent them from seeing their faults. But when a man is still, especially in the desert, then he sees his failings.' (2, p. 1.)

This stillness, this principle of non-interference, is demonstrated also in a shorter saying, and one replete with the dry and practical humour of the desert: 'There was an old man on the banks of the Jordan who went into a cave during the hot weather. Inside he found a lion who began to bare his teeth and roar. The old man said to him, "Why get annoyed? There is room enough for you and me, and if you do not like it, then go away." Not able to stand it, the lion went away' (202, p. 54). The image which best illustrates this attitude is that of the 'monk crucified', which has often been painted as a visual icon and is here described in words: 'So should the monk be: denuded·of all the things of this world, and crucified. . . . the monk stands, his arms stretched out in the form of a cross to heaven, calling on God. . . . So God leads us to victory.' (11, p.3.)

Translator's Note

The Greek text of the sayings translated here and in *The World of the Desert Fathers* is part of a manuscript written in Egypt in the fifth century and now numbered as MS Coislin 126 in the Bibliotheque Nationale, Paris. The texts were transcribed and published by M. Nau in *Le Revue de L'Orient chrétien* with a French translation of part. J. P. Migne provided a Latin version in *Patrologia Latina* 73. M. Guy has made a study of the texts in his *Recherches sur la tradition grecque des Apophthegmata Patrum*, (Subsida Hagiographica 36, Brussels 1962). Dom Lucien Regnault has indicated the location of the sayings in other collections in his *Les Sentences des Pères du désert, troisième recueil et tables* (Solesmes 1976). In this volume I have translated the Sytematic Series of sayings contained in Nau's text (see table below for detailed references) and I have numbered them from 1 to 238. The correspondence between the numbers in the Greek text and the present translation are as follows:

Nau, vol. 1908, Sayings 133–174 (pp. 47–57) = 1–42
Nau, vol. 1908, Sayings 175–215 (pp. 266–283) = 43–83
Nau, vol. 1909, Sayings 216–297 (pp. 357–379) = 84–165
Nau, vol. 1912, Sayings 298–334 (pp. 204–211) = 166–202
Nau, vol. 1913, Sayings 359–396 (pp. 137–140) = 203–238

(For more details about the manuscript in which these texts are found, see the Introduction to *The World of the Desert Fathers*.)

I should like to thank those scholars in France and England whom I have consulted about this book. I owe everything to their infectious enthusiasm and careful advice. In particular, I thank Metropolitan Anthony for his illuminating Foreword and for his continual interest in this area of monastic exploration. Several members of the Community of the Sisters of the Love of God have given time and care to criticism of my text, and several students at the Centre for Medieval and Renaissance Studies in Oxford have provided a cheerful and critical audience for several versions of the text. My aim has been to make a further section of this basic tradition of monastic spirituality available for use by English readers. The translation is therefore intended to be readable rather than pedantic, though a few Greek words, such as *accedie*, have been retained where there is no real English equivalent. A glossary of such terms is included in *Sayings of the Desert Fathers* to which this book is intended to be a companion. The minimum of interpretation has been offered, so that the reader may use the texts freely and immediately. Those who feel the need for more help in understanding them are referred to Dom Columba Stewart's Introduction in *The World of the Desert Fathers*.

The literature of the desert contained in these sayings may help towards a valid interpretation of the Gospel in our own day, in what Henri Nouwen has called 'an apocalytic situation' very similar in essence to the world in which the desert fathers lived (H. Nouwen, *The Way of the Heart*, New York, 1981, p. 9). It is no longer only 'the cell of the monk' which is 'the furnace of Babylon' and the 'pillar of cloud' (74, p. 24). A translation of these sayings may perhaps affirm that it is in that fire and that darkness that the 'Son of God is found'.

BENEDICTA WARD SLG
Oxford 1986

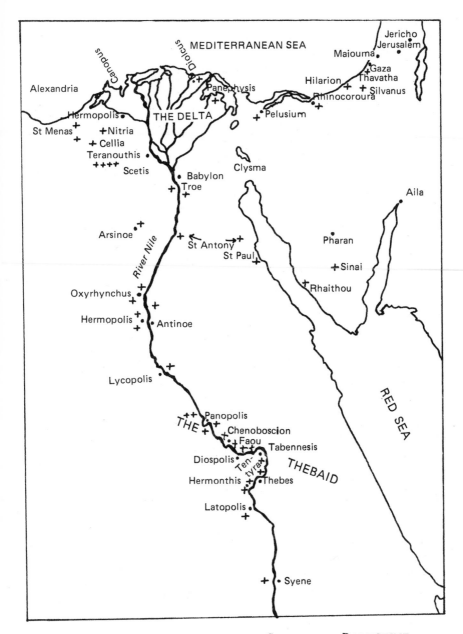

MONASTIC EGYPT, SINAI AND SOUTHERN PALESTINE

THE SAYINGS

THAT ONE SHOULD SEEK STILLNESS AND COMPUNCTION

1. An old man said, 'The monk must purchase his stillness by being despised whenever the opportunity presents itself, and by bodily labour.'

2. It was said that there were three friends who were not afraid of hard work. The first chose to reconcile those who were fighting each other, as it is said, 'Blessed are the peace-makers'. (Matt. 5.) The second chose to visit the sick. The third went to live in prayer and stillness in the desert. Now in spite of all his labours, the first could not make peace in all men's quarrels; and in his sorrow he went to him who was serving the sick, and he found him also disheartened, for he could not fulfil that commandment either. So they went together to see him who was living in the stillness of prayer. They told him their difficulties and begged him to tell them what to do. After a short silence, he poured some water into a bowl and said to them, 'Look at the water', and it was disturbed. After a little while he said to them again, 'Look how still the water is now', and as they looked into the water, they saw their own faces reflected in it as in a mirror. Then he said to them, 'It is the same for those who live among men; disturbances prevent them from seeing their faults. But when a man is still, especially in the desert, then he sees his failings.'

3. An old man told how a brother wished to go into the desert and was prevented from doing so by his mother. But he did not give up his resolution, saying, 'I want to save my soul'. In spite of many endeavours his mother could not prevent him going, and at last she let him go. He went away and lived alone, negligently frittering away his life. Now it happened that his mother died. Later on, when he was seriously ill, he had a vision and was shown the judgment, and saw his mother with those who had come to be judged. As soon as she saw him she was dumbfounded and said, 'What is this, my child, have you been condemned to this place too?

1

What about that phrase you used to use—"I want to save my soul"?' Overcome by what he had heard, he stood there, struck with amazement, having nothing to say to her. Then he heard a voice saying, 'Take him away from here, it is to another monk with the same name that I sent you, in such and such a monastery.' When the vision had come to an end he returned to himself and told those who were present about it. To strengthen belief in his words, he sent someone to the monastery of him whose name he had heard to see if the brother concerned were dead. The messenger went and found that it was so. When he had recovered from his illness, he shut himself up and started to work out his salvation; he repented and wept for what he had done before in negligence. His compunction was so great that many advised him to relax a little for fear he should suffer harm from his immoderate tears. But he did not want to relax, saying, 'If I could not endure my mother's reproach, how shall I endure shame on the day of judgment before Christ and the holy angels?'

4. An old man said, 'If it were possible, at the time of the coming of Christ after the resurrection, that men's souls should die of fear, the whole world would die of terror and confusion. What a sight, to see the heavens open and God revealed in anger and wrath, and innumerable armies of angels and, at the same time, the whole of humanity. Therefore we ought to live as having to give account to God of our way of life every day.'

5. A brother asked an old man, 'How does the fear of God come into the soul?' And the old man said, 'If a man has humility and poverty, and if he does not judge anyone, the fear of God comes to him.'

6. A brother came to see an old man and asked him, 'Abba, why is my heart so hard, and why do I not fear God?' The old man said to him, 'In my opinion, if a man bears in mind the reproaches he deserves, he will acquire the fear of God.' The brother said to him, 'What does this reproach consist of?' The old man said to him, 'In all he does, a man should restrain his own soul, saying to it, "Remember that you must come before God", and he should also say to himself, "What have I to do with the others?" I think that if someone lives in this way, the fear of God will come to him.'

7.   An old man saw someone laughing and said to him, 'We have to give account of our whole life in the presence of heaven and earth, and you are able to laugh.'

8.   An old man said, 'Just as we carry our own shadow everywhere with us, so we ought also to have tears and compunction with us wherever we are.'

9.   A brother asked an old man, 'What should I do?' And the old man said to him, 'We must weep always.' Now it happened that one of the fathers died one day, and after a long interval he returned to life, and we asked him, 'What did you see down there?' And he told us, weeping, 'Down there I heard the weeping of those who say over and over again, "Woe is me; woe is me". So we too must weep without ceasing.'

10.   A brother asked an old man saying, 'How is it that though I desire the gift of tears, of which I have heard the old men speak, they do not come? I am very worried about it.' And the old man said to him, 'The children of Israel entered the promised land after forty years. When you reach that land, you will no longer fear the battle. God, indeed, wills that you should be worried, so that you may ceaselessly desire to enter into that land.'

11.   A brother asked an old man, 'How can I be saved?' The latter took off his habit, girded his loins and raised his hands to heaven, saying, 'So should the monk be: denuded of all the things of this world, and crucified. In the contest, the athlete fights with his fists; in his thoughts, the monk stands, his arms stretched out in the form of a cross to heaven, calling on God. The athlete stands naked when fighting in a contest; the monk stands naked and stripped of all things, anointed with oil and taught by his master how to fight. So God leads us to victory.'

ABOUT SELF-CONTROL

12.   There was once a festival in Scetis, and an old man was given a cup of wine. He refused it, saying, 'Take this death away from me.' On seeing it, the others who were eating with him refused it also.

13. A brother was hungry early in the morning, and he fought his desire so as not to eat before the third hour. When the third hour came, he forced himself to wait until the sixth hour. At that time he broke his loaves and sat down to eat, then stood up again, saying to himself, 'Now wait until the ninth hour.' At the ninth hour he said the prayer and saw the power of the devil like smoke rising from his manual work, and his hunger vanished.

14. A disciple said of his abba that for twenty whole years he never lay down on his side but slept sitting on the seat on which he worked. He ate either every second or every fourth or fifth day for twenty years, and while he ate, he stretched out one hand in prayer and ate with the other. When I said to him, 'What is this about? Why do you do this, abba?' he replied, 'I set the judgment of God before my eyes, and I cannot bear it.' While we were saying our prayers one day, it happened that my memory failed me and I forgot a word of the psalms. When we had finished the prayers the old man said to me, 'When I am saying the prayers I think of myself as being on top of a burning fire, and my attention cannot stray to right or left. Where was your attention when we were saying the prayers and that word of the psalm escaped you? Don't you know that you are standing in the presence of God and speaking to God?' Another time the old man went out at night and found me sleeping in the doorway of the cell. And the old man stood there lamenting over me and saying with tears, 'Where is his attention then that he sleeps so casually?'

15. A brother came to see a very experienced old man and said to him, 'I am in trouble', and the old man said to him, 'Sit in your cell and God will give you peace.'

16. Someone brought a vessel of wine to the Cells, as first-fruits, so that a cup could be given to the brethren, and one of the brothers went up on the roof to escape, and the roof fell in. Alarmed at the noise, the others came and found him on the ground and began to blame him, saying, 'Vain fool, it served you right.' But the abbot came to his aid saying, 'Leave my son alone, he has done a good deed, and by the Lord, the roof shall never be repaired as long as I live, so that the world may know that at the Cells a roof fell in for the sake of a cup of wine.'

17.   One of the old men went to visit another old man who said to his disciple, 'Prepare a few lentils for us'—which he did—'and soak some loaves'—which he did. And they stayed until the next day, till the sixth hour, speaking of spiritual things, and the old man said to his disciple again, 'Prepare a few lentils for us, my child', and he said, 'It was ready yesterday.' So then they ate.

18.   Another old man came to see one of the Fathers, who cooked a few lentils and said to him, 'Let us say a few prayers', and the first completed the whole psalter, and the brother recited the two great prophets by heart. When morning came, the visitor went away, and they forgot the food.

19.   One of the old men was ill, and unable to take any food for many a long day. His disciple encouraged him to take more nourishing food. So he went to prepare it and brought it to him to eat. Now there was a vessel hanging there containing a little honey and another containing linseed oil, with a nasty smell, used for the light. The brother made a mistake and instead of honey, he poured that oil over the old man's food. While he was eating, the old man did not speak, but ate in silence, and his disciple urged him to eat more, and he forced himself to do so. His disciple suggested it a third time, but he refused to eat, saying, 'Truly, my child, I cannot eat any more.' The other, to give him courage, said, 'But abba, it is good; see, I am going to eat with you.' The brother ate and realized what he had done, and he threw himself at the old man's feet, saying, 'Alas, I have killed you, and you have laid the guilt of it on me by saying nothing.' The old man said, 'Do not distress yourself, if God had wished me to eat honey, you would have poured honey on it.'

20.   It was said of an old man that one day he wanted a small fig. Taking one, he held it up in front of his eyes, and not being overcome by his desire, he repented, reproaching himself for even having had this wish.

21.   A brother went to a monastery to visit his own sister who was ill. Being very exact she would not agree to see a man, not even her own brother, because he would have come into the midst of women. She sent him a message saying, 'My brother, go away and pray for me, and by the grace of Christ I shall see you in the kingdom of heaven.'

22. Meeting some nuns on the road, a monk made a detour. The superior said to him, 'If you were a perfect monk, you would not have noticed we were women.'

23. A brother brought some fresh loaves to the Cells and invited some old men to his table. Each of them stopped eating when he had had two loaves. But the brother, knowing the severity of their ascesis, bowed before them, saying, 'Eat today, for the Lord's sake, until you are satisfied.' And they ate ten more loaves. See how much less than they need, the true ascetics eat!

24. An old man was suffering from a serious illness and he was to have some dried plums, so his disciple made some stew and put them into it, and he took it to the old man and invited him to eat, saying, 'Be so good as to eat, for perhaps it will do you good.' But the old man looked long at him and said, 'Truly, I wish that God may grant me this illness for another thirty years.' Even in such a serious illness, the old man refused to eat even a little of the stew. So the brother took it and went back to his cell.

25. Another old man lived in a distant desert. It happened that a brother came to see him and found him ill. He looked after him, washed him, cooked some of the provisions he had brought, and offered them to him to eat. The old man replied, 'Truly, brother, I had forgotten that men had anything so nice.' And the brother brought him a cup of wine also. When he saw it, he began to weep, saying, 'I had not expected to drink wine before death.'

26. An old man practised the ascesis of not drinking for forty days, and if by chance it happened to be hot, he rinsed his jug, filled it with water and hung it in front of him. Questioned by a brother as to the reason for his doing this, he replied, 'It is so that my thirst may cause me greater pain, so that I may receive a greater reward from God.'

27. A brother was walking with his own mother, who was old. When they came to the river she could not cross it. Taking his cloak, her son covered his hands with it, so as not to touch his mother's body, and carrying her in this way, brought her to the other bank. And his mother said to him, 'My child, why did you cover your hands?' He said to her, 'A

woman's body is a fire, and from it comes the remembrance of other women: that is why I did that.'

28.   One of the Fathers said, 'I know a brother in the Cells who fasted in Easter week. And when they assembled together in the evening, he ran away, so as not to eat in the church, and prepared some beetroot for himself, which he ate boiled, without bread.

29.   One day the priest of Scetis went to blessed Theophilus, Archbishop of Alexandria, and when he returned to Scetis the brothers asked him, 'What is the city like?' He said to them, 'Indeed, brothers, I did not see anyone there except the Archbishop.' On learning this they were troubled, saying, 'Then has everyone been destroyed, abba?' He said to them, 'No, but the temptation to look at anyone did not overcome me.' On hearing this they were full of admiration and from this saying they drew strength to guard their eyes from wandering.

30.   Some fathers went to Alexandria one day, sent for by blessed Theophilus the Archbishop to pray there and to destroy the pagan sanctuaries. While they were eating with him they were served with veal, and ate it without noticing anything. The Archbishop, taking a piece, gave it to the old man who was beside him, saying, 'Look, here is a nice piece of meat, abba, eat it.' They replied, 'Up to now we thought we were eating vegetables, but if it is meat, we do not eat it.' And none of them ate any more.

HOW TO DEAL WITH THE WARFARE WHICH LUST AROUSES IN US

31.   A brother was attacked by lust, and the warfare was like a burning fire in his heart, day and night. The brother fought so as not to consent to these thoughts. After a long time the warfare ceased, unable to do anything because of the brother's endurance, and immediately a light came into his heart.

32.   Another brother was attacked by lust. He got up at night, went to an old man and told him his thoughts. The old man comforted him and he returned to his cell strengthened. But the struggle began again in him.

Again he went to the old man. And he did this many times. The old man did not reproach him but spoke to him of what might help him, saying to him, 'Do not give way, but rather come every time the demon wars against you.' And the brother treated the demon with contempt, and he disappeared when he was despised. For, truly, nothing annoys the demon of lust like revealing his works, and nothing pleases him like concealing one's thoughts.

33.   A brother was attacked by lust, and he fought and intensified his ascesis, guarding his thoughts so as not to consent to those desires. Later he came to the church and revealed the matter to everyone. And the commandment was given to all to do penance for that week for his sake, and to pray to God—and the warfare ceased.

34.   Concerning the temptation to lust, one of the old men, a hermit, said, 'Do you wish to be saved after death? Go, and work; go, and give yourself hardship; go, seek and you shall find; watch and knock, and it will be opened to you. In the world there are those who fight in the arena and endure, and although they are given many blows, they receive the crown. Often, indeed, a single athlete is struck by two others and, invigorated by the blows, he overcomes those who are hitting him. Do you see what strength he gains by bodily exercise? Act with vigour, therefore, and God will fight for you against the enemy.'

35.   Against the same thought, another old man said, 'Be like him who passes through the market place in front of an inn and breathes the smell of cooking and roasting. If he enjoys it, he goes inside to eat some of it; if not, he only inhales the smell in passing and goes on his way. It is the same for you: avoid the bad smell. Wake up and pray, saying, "Son of God, help me." Do this for other temptations also. For we do not have to uproot the passions, but resist them.'

36.   A brother asked an old man, 'If a monk succumbs to temptation he is grieved because he falls from perfection to a lower level, and he struggles to rise again; while he who comes from the world makes progress as a beginner.' And the old man answered him, 'The monk who succumbs to temptation is like a house which collapses. If he is watchful in his thoughts, he finds much material for building the house which collapsed—

foundations, stones, wood—and he is able to make more rapid progress than he who has not dug and laid foundations and who does not possess any materials but only has the hope that the house will be finished one day. So it is for him who after a long monastic training succumbs to temptation: if he repents he finds various materials—meditation, psalmody, and manual work—these are the foundations. But the beginner must first learn all this, while the monk can return to his former level.'

37. A brother overcome by lust went to see a great old man and besought him, saying, 'Be so good as to pray for me, for I am overcome by lust.' And the old man prayed to God for him. A second time he went to the old man and said the same thing, and once more the old man did not omit to beseech God for him, saying, 'Lord, reveal to me the manner of life of this brother and whence comes this action of the devil, for I have already besought you and he has not found peace'. Then God revealed this to him about the brother: he saw him sitting with the spirit of lust beside him and an angel, sent to his aid, was standing beside him and becoming angry with him because he did not fall down before God but, taking pleasure in his thoughts, delivered up his spirit completely to the action of the devil. So the old man knew that the cause came from the brother, and he told him, 'It is you who are consenting to your thoughts.' Then he taught him how to resist thoughts, and the brother, restored by the old man's prayer and teaching, found rest.

38. The disciple of a great old man was once attacked by lust. The old man, seeing it in his prayer, said to him, 'Do you want me to ask God to relieve you of this battle?' The other said, 'Abba, I see that I am afflicted, but I see that this affliction is producing fruit in me; therefore ask God to give me endurance to bear it.' And his abba said to him, 'Today I know you surpass me in perfection.'

39. It was said of an old man that he went down to Scetis, and that he still had a son who was quite small and did not know what a woman was. Now when he became a man, the demons showed him the forms of women, and he told his father, who was astonished at it. Once when he went up to Egypt with his father and saw women, he said to his father, 'Abba, these are the people who came to me at night in Scetis.' And his father said to him, 'These people are village monks, my child, and they

9

wear different clothing from hermits.' The old man was astonished at the way the demons in the desert had shown him forms of women; and immediately they returned to their cells.

40. A brother at Scetis was a good fighter. The enemy suggested the remembrance of a very beautiful woman to him and he was much afflicted by it. Providentially, another brother who went to Scetis from Egypt said to him, while they were speaking together, 'The wife of so and so is dead.' Now it was the woman about whom the ascetic had experienced the conflict. When he heard this, he took his cloak and went to open her tomb by night; he soaked the cloak in the decomposing body. Then he returned to his cell bringing this bad smell with him, and he strove against his thoughts, saying, 'Here is the desire you are seeking—you have it—be satisfied.' And he chastised himself by means of that bad smell until the warfare in him ceased.

41. Someone came to Scetis one day to become a monk. He had his son, who was scarcely weaned, with him. When the boy became a young man, the battles against him began, and he said to his father, 'I am returning to the world for I cannot endure the warfare.' His father persevered, encouraging him, but the young man said again, 'Abba, I cannot do any more, let me go.' And his father said to him, 'My child, listen to me just once more. Take forty measures of bread and palm leaves for forty days' work with you, and go to the interior desert, and stay there for forty days; and may the Lord's will be done.' He obeyed his father, arose, went into the desert and stayed there in hardship, plaiting the palm leaves and eating dry bread. He stayed there for twenty days; then he saw the power of the devil coming towards him: it appeared to him like an Ethiopian woman smelling so vile that he could not bear it. So he drove her away, and she said to him, 'I usually seem to be pleasant to the hearts of men, but because of your obedience and your labour, God has not let you be deceived and he has revealed my bad smell to you.' So rising up and giving thanks to God he returned to his father and said, 'I no longer wish to go back to the world, abba, for I have seen its power and its bad smell.' Now what had happened had been revealed to his father, and he said to him, 'If you had remained forty days and kept my commandment you would have seen a greater vision.'

42.   They said of one of the Fathers who had lived in the world that he suffered temptation through remembering his own wife. So he made this known to the Fathers. Knowing that he was a hard worker and did more than people said of him, they imposed such rules on him that his body became so weak that he could no longer stand up. By the Providence of God, a Father from foreign parts came to Scetis and coming to his cell and seeing it open he went on further, surprised that no one came to meet him. Then he turned round and knocked, saying to himself, 'Perhaps the brother is ill.' He knocked, entered, and finding him very weak, said to him, 'What is the matter with you, Father?' And he told him, 'I lived in the world, and now the enemy wars against me through the thought of my wife, and I told the Fathers and they imposed various rules on me. I am exhausted by carrying them out, and the warfare increases.' When he heard this, the old man was grieved at it and said to him, 'The Fathers are able men who have done well in imposing these rules on you, but if you will hear me in my humility, give all this up, and take a little food at the proper time, say a few prayers, and give your anxiety over to the Lord. With the hardships which you are practising you are not able to overcome this difficulty. Truly, our body is like a cloak: if you take care of it, it lasts, but if you neglect it, it is damaged.' The other listened, and acted in this way, and in a few days the warfare ceased.

43.   There was an anchorite who had settled in the desert in the district of Antinoë and was progressing in virtue. Many were edified by his words and deeds. The enemy was jealous of his goodness, as he is wont to be of all virtuous men, and under the guise of piety suggested the following thought to him, 'You should not let yourself be served by another, but you ought to serve others; since you do not do that, at least serve yourself. So go and sell your baskets and buy whatsoever you need, then return at once to your anchoritic life without being a burden to anyone.' This is what that deceiver, jealous of his silent prayer, his attention to God, and the help many received from him, suggested. Truly, the enemy strove in all ways to take him captive. Convinced by a thought which he believed to be good, he went down to his monastery, this anchorite whom at that time everyone admired. He was really without experience of the great astuteness of the demon who was setting snares for him, although he was an anchorite, known and of repute.

After a long time, he met a woman and since he was weakened by his carelessness, he went to a desert place, accompanied by the enemy, and he sinned beside the river. When he realized how the enemy was rejoicing at his fall, he began to despair of himself for having so greatly grieved the Spirit of God, the angels, and the holy Fathers, many of whom, even in the cities, had overcome the enemy. Unable to think of anyone like himself, he was filled with sadness, not remembering that God grants strength to those who firmly hope in him. Because he could not see how his sin could be healed, he wanted to throw himself into the river and die there. The great torment of his soul made his body ill, and if the God of mercy had not helped him, he would have died without repentance, to the great delight of the enemy. Returning at last to his senses, he thought of trying to endure greater affliction in suffering. So he returned to the monastery and closed his cell door, and he wept, as it behoves us to weep over a dead body, beseeching God. By fasting and watching in affliction, his body grew weak, yet he did not feel he had done enough penance. Brothers often came to see him for their spiritual benefit, and when they knocked on the door, he said he could not open to them. 'I have given my word', he said, 'to do penance seriously for a year.' And he added, 'Pray for me', not knowing how else to reply so as not to shock his listeners, for he was of great repute amongst them and considered as a great monk. So he spent the whole year in severe penance.

When the day of the Pasch came, on the night of the holy resurrection, he took a new lamp and prepared it, putting in a new wick and covering it. In the evening he began to pray, saying, 'O merciful and compassionate God, you will that even the barbarians should be saved and come to the knowledge of the truth, I flee to you, Saviour of souls. Have pity on me, who, to the delight of the enemy, have so grieved you, and who at present am dead through having obeyed the enemy. Master, you have mercy on the godless and those who are without mercy, and you have taught us to be merciful to others—have compassion on my weakness. For to you nothing is impossible. My soul deserves hell. Have pity on me, for you are gracious to your creatures, for on the day of the resurrection, you willed to awaken even the bodies which no longer have life. Hear me, Lord, for my spirit and my unhappy soul fail me. Even my body, which I have defiled, falls into decay, and I am no longer able to live because of my dread of you. Instead of believing that my sin would be pardoned through penitence, I committed a double sin by my unfaithfulness. Revive me, for I am crushed, and command that this lamp may be kindled by your fire, that I may receive the assurance of your mercy, and know that in your mercy you have forgiven me. I will keep your commandments all the days of my life which you grant me, and I will no more depart from your fear, but I will serve you faithfully, even better than before.'

Having uttered these words with many tears on the night of the resurrection, he got up to see if the lamp was alight. When he uncovered it and saw that it was not alight, he made a prostration again before the Lord and besought him, saying, 'Lord, I know there are difficulties in the way of my being crowned, for I have not watched my steps, thinking rather of the pleasures of the flesh than of the punishment of blasphemers. Spare me, Lord, for once more I confess your goodness and my baseness before you, in the presence of all your angels and the saints; if it were not a matter for scandal, I would confess it also before men. Accordingly, have mercy on me, that I may be able to teach mercy to others. Even so, Lord, revive me.' Having prayed thus three times, he was heard. Getting up, he found the lamp was burning brightly. Filled with hope, he was strengthened by the joy of his heart and he rejoiced, wondering at the grace God had granted him in giving him this sign. He said, 'Unworthy of this life as I am, you have had mercy on me through this great and ineffable sign.' He remained thus, prolonging his confession, and the day dawned and he rejoiced in the Lord without remembering bodily food. He preserved the light of this lamp all the days of his life, pouring oil into it and feeding it for fear lest it should go out. Thus the divine Spirit dwelt in him again, and he became a sign for all, humble in his witness to the Lord and his acknowledgment of him. When he came to the point of delivering up his soul, this was revealed to him several days beforehand.

44.   An old man dwelt in a distant desert, and he had a relative who had wanted to visit him for many years. Having made enquiries about the place where he dwelt, she arose and set out on the road to the desert; meeting a camel caravan, she penetrated into the desert with it. Now she was drawn by the devil. Having arrived at the old man's door, she made herself known by signs, saying, 'I am your relation', and she stayed beside him. The old man was attacked, and he sinned with her. Now there was another anchorite who had settled in a lower region. He had filled his jug with water, and at meal time he knocked the jug over, and by the providence of God he said to himself, 'I will go to the desert and tell the old man.' He got up and went out. When evening came, he went to sleep by

13

the roadside in a pagan temple, and during the night he heard the demons saying, 'We have drawn the anchorite into fornication this night.' When he heard this he was grieved, and going to the old man found him disheartened, and he said to him, 'What shall I do, abba, for I filled my jug with water, and at meal time I knocked it over?' And the old man said to him, 'You have come to consult me because your jug fell over, but what shall I do, for this night I fell into fornication?' The other said, 'I know.' He said to him, 'How do you know?' The other said, 'As I was asleep in the temple I heard the demons talking about you.' And the old man said, 'I am going back to the world.' The other encouraged him, saying, 'No, father, stay where you are; only send the woman away from here, for this has happened through the contrivance of the enemy.' And he listened to him and remained, intensifying his way of life with tears until he recovered his former state.

45. A brother questioned an old man, 'If it happens that someone gives way to temptation in consequence of some impulse or other, what may befall him through those who are shocked by it?' He replied, 'In an Egyptian monastery there was a famous deacon. Now an official, prosecuted by the judge, came to the monastery with his whole family. Driven by the Evil One, the deacon sinned with the man's wife, and he became a cause of scorn to everyone. So he went to an old man among his friends and made the matter known to him. Now the old man had a sort of crypt behind his cell, and the deacon begged him, "Bury me there alive, and tell no one." He went into this dark place and did strict penance.

Some time later, the river did not flood, and while everyone was saying litanies, it was revealed to one of the saints that the water would not rise unless a certain deacon who was hidden with a certain monk came. On learning this they were filled with astonishment and went to bring the deacon out from the place where he was. And he prayed, and the water rose, and those who before had been shocked were much more edified at his repentance, and they gave glory to God.

46. An old man said, 'Many, tempted by bodily pleasures, do not defile their bodies but, committing fornication in thought, they are fornicators in their souls while preserving their bodies unstained. So it is good, my friends, to do that which is written, that each one should guard his heart with great care.'

14

47.   Two brothers went to market to sell the things they had made. The first fell into fornication as soon as he separated from his companion. He met his brother who said to him, 'My brother, let us go to our cell', but he replied, 'I am not going'. The other persisted, saying, 'My brother, why not?' He said, 'Because when you had left me, I fell into fornication.' His brother, wishing to win him over, said to him, 'The same thing happened to me, too, when you left me; come, let us go and do strict penance and God will forgive us.' They went to tell the old men what had happened to them, and the old men gave them commandments for doing penance. Then one of the brothers did penance for the other as though he had sinned himself. But God, seeing the affliction he was giving himself for love's sake, made known to one of the old men, after some days, that because of the great love of the brother who had not sinned, he had forgiven the one who had sinned. See what it is to give one's soul for one's brother.

48.   One day a brother came to see an old man and said to him, 'My brother wears me out going about here and there, and I am afflicted by it.' And the old man encouraged him, saying, 'Bear with your brother, and God, seeing your forbearance, will take care of you. Truly, one does not readily care for someone through hardness, just as a demon does not drive a demon away; but, rather, care for him through goodness, for our God cares for men by encouraging them.'

And he told him this: 'In the Thebaid there were two brothers. One being attacked by lust, said to the other, "I am going into the world", and the other began to weep, saying, "My brother, I will not let you go and lose the fruit of your labour and your virginity." But the other did not let himself be persuaded, saying, "I am not staying here, I am going. Either go with me and I shall return later with you, or let me go and I shall stay in the world." The brother went to tell all this to a great old man who said to him, "Go with him, and because of the labour you are giving yourself, God will not let him fall." They arose and returned to the world, but as they were approaching the village, God, seeing his labour, withdrew the warfare from his brother, who said to him, "Let us go back to the desert, my brother, for I have realized I shall not get any profit from my sin." And they returned to their cells uninjured.

49   A brother attacked by the demon went to see an old man and said to him, 'Those two brothers sleep together'. And the old man saw

that he was mocked by the demons, and he sent someone to call them. When evening came, he spread a mat for the two brothers and covered them with a single covering, saying, 'The children of God are saints'; and he said to his disciple, 'Shut this brother in the cell outside because it is he who has this temptation in himself.'

50.   A brother said to an old man, 'What shall I do? Evil thoughts are killing me.' The old man said to him, 'When a mother wishes to wean her child, she rubs her breast with squills, and when the child comes to suck as usual, the bitterness repels it. Do you likewise use squills.' The brother said to him, 'But what are the squills I ought to use?' And the old man said to him, 'The remembrance of death and the punishments of the age to come.'

51.   The same brother asked another old man about the same thought. And the old man said to him, 'I myself have never had to fight against such a thing.' And the brother was shocked at it and went to see another old man, saying to him, 'This is what a certain old man said to me, and I am shocked at it, for he has spoken beyond nature.' The second old man said to him, 'The man of God has not said that to you simply on the surface; but arise, go and kneel before him, so that he may tell you the meaning of his saying.' So the brother arose and went to see the first old man, and he knelt before him and said, 'Forgive me, abba, for I have acted like a fool in going away hurriedly, and I beg you to tell me how it is you have never had to fight against lust.' The old man said, 'Since I became a monk, I have never eaten bread to satiety, nor drunk water, nor slept to satiety, and attention to these things has so weighed me down that it has not let me feel the warfare of which you are speaking.' And the brother went away edified.

52.   A brother asked one of the Fathers, 'What shall I do? My thoughts are always turned to lust without allowing me an hour's respite, and my soul is tormented by it.' He said to him, 'Every time the demons suggest these thoughts to you, do not argue with them. For the activity of demons always is to suggest, and suggestions are not sins, for they cannot compel; but it rests with you to welcome them, or not to welcome them. Do you know what the Midianites did? They adorned their daughters and presented them to the Israelites. They did not compel anyone, but those

who consented, sinned with them, while the others were enraged and put them to death. It is the same with thoughts.' The brother answered the old man, 'What shall I do, then, for I am weak and passion overcomes me?' He said to him, 'Watch your thoughts, and every time they begin to say something to you, do not answer them but rise and pray; kneel down, saying, "Son of God, have mercy on me".' Then the brother said to him, 'Look, abba, I meditate, and there is no compunction in my heart because I do not understand the meaning of the words.' The other said to him, 'Be content to meditate. Indeed, I have learned that Abba Poemen and many other Fathers uttered the following saying, 'The magician does not understand the meaning of the words which he pronounces, but the wild animal who hears it understands, submits, and bows to it. So it is with us also: even if we do not understand the meaning of the words we are saying, when the demons hear them, they take fright and go away.'

53. The old men used to say that the temptation to lust is like a hook. If it is suggested to us and we do not let ourselves be overcome by it, it is easily cut off; but if, once it is presented, we take pleasure in it and let ourselves be overcome, it transforms itself and becomes like iron and is difficult to cut off. Thus discernment is needed about these thoughts, because for those who allow themselves to be seduced there is no hope of salvation, whereas crowns are prepared for the others.

54. Two brothers who were attacked by lust went away to get married. Later on they said to one another, 'What have we gained by leaving the angelic order and coming to this impurity? In the end we shall suffer fire and punishment. Let us then return to the desert and repent.' So they returned and asked the Fathers to give them a penance, confessing what they had done. The old men imposed seclusion for a year on them, giving to each one the same amount of bread and water. Now they were alike physically. When the time of penitence was fulfilled, they came out, and the Fathers saw the first was pale and humbled while the other looked well, with a clear countenance. They were surprised, for they had had the same food. They asked the one who was humbled, 'How did you get on with your thoughts in the cell?' He said, 'I thought of the evil I had done and the judgment to which I was going, and the fear of it made my bones cleave to my flesh.' Then they asked the other, 'What did you think in your heart in your cell?' He said, 'I thanked God for having taken

me out of the impurity of the world to judgment, and for having led me to this way of life in Jesus Christ, and I rejoiced in the remembrance of God.' Then the old men said, 'In the eyes of God, the penitence of the two men is of equal value.'

55.   There was an old man in Scetis who fell seriously ill. The brothers cared for him and, seeing the inconvenience it caused them, the old man said, 'I will go away to Egypt so as not to harm the brothers.' But Abba Moses said to him, 'Do not go away, for you will fall into lust.' The other was annoyed and said, 'My body is dead, so how can you say that?' And he left for Egypt. When they heard of it, people brought him many gifts and a devout virgin came to look after him. Shortly after, when he had recovered, he sinned with her and she became pregnant. People said to her, 'How did this happen?' She said, 'By the old man.' They did not believe it until the old man said, 'It is I who am to blame, but look after the child which she has brought into the world.'

When the child was weaned, one day when there was a feast in Scetis, the old man came down, carrying the child on his shoulder, and he went into the church in the presence of all the people. The congregation began to weep when they saw him, and he said to the brothers, 'Do you see this child? He is the son of disobedience. Be careful, then, my brothers, for in my old age I have done this, and pray for me.' Then, going to his cell, he resumed his former manner of life.

56.   A brother was severely tempted by the demon of lust. In fact, four demons, under the appearance of very beautiful women, spent forty days attacking him to bring him to the shame of intercourse. But he fought courageously and was not overcome, and seeing his successful warfare, God allowed him to experience no more the flames of sensuality.

57.   In Lower Egypt there was an anchorite who was well-known because he dwelt in a solitary cell in the desert. Now by the power of Satan, a shameless woman who had heard of him said to some young men, 'What would you give me if I could cause your anchorite to fall?' They agreed to give her something of value. In the evening she went out and came to his cell as though she had lost her way, and when she knocked the anchorite came out. When he saw her he was troubled and said, 'How have you come here?' Weeping, she said, 'I came here because I have lost my

way.' Filled with compassion, he made her come into the entry, and he returned to his cell and shut it, but the unfortunate creature began to cry out, 'Abba, the wild animals are eating me.' He was uneasy again, but fearing the judgment of God, he said, 'What is the source of this hardness of mine?' and he opened the door and made her come inside. Then the devil attempted to attack him with his arrows. Pondering the warfare of the enemy, he said, 'The ways of the enemy are darkness, whereas the Son of God is light', and he rose and lit the lamp. Burning with desire, he said, 'Those who commit such acts go to the punishment; try then, and see if you can bear the everlasting fire', and he put his finger into the lamp and burnt it without feeling it, so extreme was the sensual flame. He went on doing this until morning, burning all his fingers. The unfortunate woman, seeing what he was doing, was petrified with fear. In the morning the young men came to see the anchorite and said to him, 'Did a woman come here last night?' He said, 'Yes, she is inside, asleep.' They entered and found her dead, and they said to him, 'Abba, she is dead'. Then, uncovering his hands, he showed them to them, saying, 'Look what the daughter of the devil has done to me: she has destroyed my fingers', and he told them what had happened and said, 'It is written, "Do not render evil for evil" ', and he prayed and awoke her, and she went away and lived wisely the rest of her life.

58.   A brother was attacked by the demon of lust. Now it happened that he went through an Egyptian village where he saw the daughter of a priest of the pagans. He fell in love with her and said to her father, 'Give her to me as my wife'. The other replied, 'I cannot give her to you without the authority of my god', and he went to the demon and said to him, 'Here is a monk who has come, wanting my daughter. Shall I give her to him?' The demon replied, 'Ask him if he will deny his God, his baptism, and his promises as a monk.' The monk agreed to this, and immediately he saw, as it were, a dove coming out of his mouth which flew away to the heavens. Then the priest went to the demon and said to him, 'Yes, he has agreed to these three things.' Then the devil replied, 'Do not give him your daughter to wife, for his God has not gone from him and continues to help him.' The priest went and said to him, 'I cannot give her to you, for your God aids you and has not turned from you.' When he heard these words, the brother said to himself, 'God has shown me so great goodness, wretch that I am, even though I have denied Him, together with my

baptism and promises as a monk. God, who is good, continues even now to come to my aid!' So he came to his senses, and became watchful, and went to the desert to visit a great old man to tell him about the affair. The old man replied, 'Stay here with me in the cave, and fast for three consecutive weeks, and I will intercede for you to God', and the old man laboured for the brother and besought God, saying, 'Lord, I beseech you, grant me this soul and receive his repentance', and God heard him. When one week was over, the old man went to visit the brother and asked him, 'Have you seen anything?' The brother replied, 'Yes, I have seen a dove, high up in the heavens, facing towards my head.' And the old man replied, 'Give heed to yourself and implore God strenuously.' After the second week the old man went to see the brother and asked him, 'Have you seen anything?' He replied, 'I have seen the dove close to my head', and the old man encouraged him, 'Be watchful and pray.' As soon as the third week was completed, the old man sent to see him once again and asked him, 'Have you seen anything else?' He said, 'I have seen the dove coming and standing on my head, and I put out my hand to take her, and the dove took wing and entered into my mouth.' Then the old man gave thanks to God and said to the brother, 'See, God has accepted your repentance; henceforth, watch yourself.' And the brother replied, 'From now on, abba, I shall stay with you till my death.'

59.　One of the old men of the Thebaid used to tell the following story: 'I was the son of a pagan priest. When I was small I would sit and watch my father who often went to sacrifice to the idol. Once, going in behind him in secret, I saw Satan and all his army standing beside him; and behold, one of the chief devils came to bow before him. Satan said, "Where have you come from?" He answered, "I was in a certain place and made much blood flow, and I have come to tell you about it." Satan asked, "How long did it take you to do this?" He replied, "Thirty days." Then Satan commanded him to be flogged, saying, "In so long a time have you done only that?" And behold, another demon came to bow before him. He asked him, "And you, where have you come from?" The demon replied, "I was on the sea, and I made the waves rise, and small craft foundered, and I have killed many people, and I have come to inform you of it." He said to him, "How long did it take you to do this?" and the demon said, "Twenty days". Satan commanded that he also should be flogged, saying, "That is because in such a long time you have only done this." Now a third demon came to bow before him. He asked, "And where have you come from?" The demon replied, "There was a marriage in a certain village, and I stirred up a riot, and I have made much blood flow, killing the bride and bridegroom, and I have come to inform you." He asked him, "How long have you taken to do this?" and he replied, "Ten days." And Satan commanded that he also should be flogged because he had taken too long. After this another demon came to bow before him. He asked, "And where have you come from?" He said, "I was in the desert forty years fighting against a monk, and this night I made him fall into fornication." When he heard this, Satan arose, embraced him, and put the crown he was wearing on his head and made him sit on his throne, saying, "You have been able to do a very great deed!" ' The old man said, 'Seeing this, I said to myself, "Truly, it is a great contest, this contest of the monks", and with God assisting me for my salvation, I went away and became a monk.'

NARRATIVES LEADING US TO ENDURANCE AND STABILITY

60. An old man said, 'When trials come to a man, afflictions from all directions increase to cause him to become faint-hearted and to make him complain.' And the old man related the following story, 'At the Cells there was a brother upon whom trials fell. When the others saw him, they did not greet him or take him into their cells, and when he needed bread, no one supplied him with any, and when he returned from the harvest, no one invited him to church for the *agape* as was customary. Coming back from the harvest once he had not even any bread in his cell, and he thanked God for all this. Seeing his endurance, God withdrew the warfare of this trial from him. Someone came and knocked on his door, with a camel laden with bread, coming from Egypt. But the brother began to weep and to say, 'Lord, was I not worthy to bear a little affliction for your name's sake?' And when the trial was over, the brethren retained him in their cells and welcomed him in the church.'

61. Some brethren went to the desert to visit a great old man, and they said to him, 'Abba, why did you come here to endure such hardship?' And the old man said, 'The whole time of the hardship I give myself here does not equal a single day of punishment.'

62.   An old man said, 'Our predecessors did not readily change their dwelling except for the three following reasons: if there happened to be someone who had a complaint against them and if in spite of all their efforts they had not been able to settle it; or if they were praised by the multitude; or if they risked falling into fornication.'

63.   A brother asked an old man, 'What shall I do? For my thoughts trouble me, saying, "You can neither fast nor work, at least go and visit the sick, for this also is charity".' The old man said to him, 'Go, eat, drink, sleep, only do not leave your cell, for you must realize that it is endurance in the cell that leads the monk to his full stature.' For three days the brother did this, then he suffered from *accidie*. Finding some palm leaves, he trimmed them and the next day began to plait them, and as he was labouring he said, 'Here are some more palm leaves, I will prepare them and then I will eat'. When he had finished the palm leaves he said, 'I will read a little and then I will eat', and when he had done some reading, he said, 'I will chant some psalms, then I shall eat in peace.' Thus, by the help of God, he advanced little by little till he reached his full stature, and taking courage against his temptations, he overcome them.

64.   Someone asked an old man, 'Why do I suffer from *accidie* when I am sitting in my cell?' And he replied, 'Because you do not clearly see either the quiet to be hoped for, or the punishment to come. For if you did see them clearly, one would be able to fill your cell with vermin till they came up to your neck and you would endure it without *accidie*.'

65.   The brethren begged one of the old men to curb his great ascetic efforts, and he replied to them, 'I tell you, my children, that Abraham, when he saw the great gifts of God, had to repent for not having striven beforehand.'

66.   A brother questioned an old man, saying, 'My thoughts wander and I am troubled by this.' The old man said to him, 'Remain sitting in your cell and your thoughts will come to rest. For truly, just as when the she-ass is tied her colt runs here and there but always comes back to his mother wherever she is, so it is with the thoughts of him who for God's sake remains steadfast in his cell: even if they wander a little they will always come back to him.'

67.   An old man lived in the desert in a cell twelve miles from the water. Every time he went to draw water he toiled and said, 'What good is this labour? I will go and live close to the water.' Saying this, he turned back and saw someone who was going with him and counting his steps and he asked, 'Who are you?' He said, 'I am the angel of the Lord, and I have been sent to count your steps and to give you your reward.' When he heard this, the old man was reassured and became more courageous, and he went and settled five miles further off.

68.   The Fathers used to say, 'If a temptation comes to you in the place where you live, do not leave the place at the time of temptation, for wherever you go you will find that which you fled from there before you. But stay until the temptation is past, that your departure may not cause offence and may be done in peace, and then you will not cause any distress amongst those who dwell in the place.'

69.   There was a brother who was a *hesychast* in a monastery, and he often got angry. So he said within himself, 'I will go and live apart, alone, and the fact of having nothing to do with anyone will assuage my passion.' So he went away and lived in solitude in a cave. Now one day when he had filled his jug with water he put it on the ground, and suddenly it fell over. He picked it up, filled it, and it fell over again. Having filled it a third time, he put it down and it fell over again. He was furious and picked it up and broke it. Coming to his senses, he recognized that he had been deceived by the enemy, and he said, 'Since I have been overcome, even after withdrawing into solitude, I will go back to the monastery, for everywhere there is warfare, endurance, and the help of God.' So he arose and returned to his place.

70.   A brother asked an old man, 'What shall I do, father, for I am not acting at all like a monk, but I eat, drink, and sleep carelessly; and I have evil thoughts and I am in great trouble, passing from one work to another and from one thought to another?' The old man said, 'Sit in your cell and do the little you can untroubled. For I think the little you can do now is of equal value to the great deeds which Abba Antony accomplished on the mountain, and I believe that by remaining sitting in your cell for the name of God, and guarding your conscience, you also will find the place where Abba Antony is.'

71.   An old man was asked, 'How can a fervent brother not be shocked when he sees others returning to the world?' And he said, 'Watch the dogs who chase hares. When one of them has seen a hare he pursues it until he catches it, without being concerned with anything else; the others, seeing the dog launched in pursuit, run with it for a short time, and soon come back. Only the one who has seen the hare follows it till he catches it, not letting himself be turned from his course by those who go back, and not caring about the ravines, rocks, and undergrowth. So it is with him who seeks Christ as Master: ever mindful of the Cross, he cares for none of the scandals that occur, till he reaches the Crucified.'

72.   An old man said, 'Just as a tree cannot bring forth fruit if it is always being transplanted, so the monk who is always going from one place to another is not able to bring forth virtue.

73.   A brother who was weighed down with the temptation to leave the monastery informed his abba, who said to him, 'Go, and sit in your cell and give your body in pledge to the walls of the cell, and do not come out of it. Let your imagination think what it likes, only do not let your body leave the cell.'

74.   An old man said, 'The monk's cell is like the furnace of Babylon where the three children found the Son of God, and it is like the pillar of cloud where God spoke with Moses.'

75.   A brother spent nine years fighting against the temptation to leave the monastery. Every morning he prepared his cloak to go away, and when evening came he said within himself, 'Tomorrow I am going to leave these parts.' In the morning he would say, 'Let us strive to hold out again today for the Lord's sake.' And when he had acted in this way for nine years, God took all temptation from him and he was at peace.

76.   A brother fell when he was tempted, and in his distress he gave up his monastic rule. Though he wanted to take it up again, he was prevented by his distress, and he said within himself, 'When shall I be able to be as I was before?' In his discouragement he had not the strength to undertake monastic work, so he went to visit an old man and told him about himself. And when the old man learnt of his distress, he suggested

the following example to him, 'A man had a plot of land, and through negligence it became waste land and was full of weeds and brambles. Later he wanted to cultivate it and said to his son, "Go, and weed the ground", and the son, going to weed it, saw the amount of brambles and despaired, saying to himself, "When shall I have uprooted and reclaimed all that?" So he lay down and went to sleep for several days. Later his father came to see what he had done and found he had done nothing at all. He said to him, "Why have you done nothing so far?" He replied, "Father, when I began to look and saw the amount of weeds and brambles I altered my resolution, and in my distress, I lay down on the ground." His father said to him, "My child, do just the surface of the bed every day, and so your work will make progress and you will not be discouraged." When he heard this he did so, and in a short while the plot was weeded. So it is for you, brother, work a little without giving way and by his grace God will re-establish you in your former way of life.' At these words the brother settled down with perseverance and did as the old man had taught him, and by the grace of Christ he found peace.

77.   There was an old man who was constantly ill. Now it happened that he was without suffering for one year, and he was vexed and wept, saying, 'God has forsaken me and has not visited me.'

78.   An old man said, 'For nine years a brother was tempted in thought to the point of despairing of his salvation, and being scrupulous he condemned himself, saying, "I have lost my soul, and since I am lost I shall go back to the world". But while he was on the way, a voice came to him on the road, which said, "These nine years during which you have been tempted have been crowns for you; go back to your place, and I will allay these thoughts." Understand that it is not good for someone to despair of himself because of his temptations; rather, temptations procure crowns for us if we use them well.'

79.   There was an old man in the Thebaid who lived in a cave and who had an experienced disciple. Now it was the old man's custom to give him some advice for his benefit every evening and then to say a prayer and send him to bed. One day, knowing the old man's great *ascesis*, some devout seculars went to see him and he edified them. When they had gone, the old man sat down again in the evening, according to custom, and

admonished the brother, but while he was speaking to him, he fell asleep. The brother waited for the old man to wake up and say the prayer. Having sat for a long time, when the old man did not awaken, he was troubled by the thought of going to rest without being sent, but he did violence to himself, resisted the thought, and remained. Later the same thought assailed him, but he did not go away, and thus he resisted this temptation seven times. After this, the night being well advanced, the old man awoke and found him sitting beside him. He said to him, 'Haven't you gone yet?' He said, 'No, abba, for you haven't sent me.' And the old man said, 'Why did you not wake me up?' He said, 'I did not dare to wake you, so as not to disturb you.'

They arose and recited the dawn prayers, and after the synaxis the old man dismissed the brother and sat down alone. At that time he was rapt in ecstasy, and someone showed him a wonderful place where there was a throne and on the throne seven crowns. He asked him who was showing him, 'Whose is that?' He said to him, 'It is your disciple's; God has granted this place and the throne to him because of his obedience; as for the seven crowns, he wore them this night.' When he heard this the old man was filled with wonder, and in his astonishment he called the brother and said to him, 'Tell me what you have done this night'. The other said, 'Forgive me, abba, I have done nothing.' Thinking that through humility he did not want to say anything, the old man said to him, 'I will not let you go till you have told me what you have done and what you have thought this night.' The brother, who thought he had not done anything, did not know what to say. So he said to his father, 'Abba, I have done nothing except this: seven times I was oppressed by the thought of going away before you had dismissed me, and I did not go.' When he heard this the old man understood that God had crowned him as many times as he had resisted the temptation. He said nothing to the brother, but he related it to the spiritual Fathers for their benefit, so that we may know that God grants us crowns even for small things. Truly it is good to constrain oneself for God's sake. In truth the kingdom of heaven suffers violence, and the violent take possession of it. (Matt. 11:12.)

80.   Once an old man in Scetis was ill. He lived alone and had no one to serve him. He got up and ate what he had in the cell. He lived in this way for many days, and no one came to see him. After thirty days, during which no one came to visit him, God sent an angel to serve him. When he

had been there for seven days, the Fathers remembered the old man and said, 'Perhaps this old man is dead?' When they came to knock on his door, the angel went away. From inside, the old man cried out, saying, 'Go away from here, my brothers.' Forcing the door, they entered, and asked him why he had cried out. He said to them, 'There were thirty days when I was in pain and no one came to visit me, and seven days ago God sent an angel to serve me, but when you came he went away from me.' When he had said this, he died. The brothers were very astonished and gave glory to God because the Lord does not forsake those who hope in him.

81. An old man said, 'If a bodily illness comes to you, do not be disturbed. For truly, if your Master wants you to be sick in body, who are you to resist? Will he not himself care for you in all things? Can you live without him? Live without bitterness, then, and beg him to supply you with what is necessary. This is what his will is, that you should remain in patience, eating the charity which is brought you.'

82. One of the fathers related this: 'Once when I was at Oxyrhyncus, some poor people came on Saturday evening to receive charity. We were lying down, and there was one of them who only had a single mat, half underneath and half on top of him. Now it was cold, and when I went out for my natural needs, I heard his teeth chattering because of the severe cold, and he was encouraging himself, saying, "I thank you, Lord: how many rich people are in prison wearing irons at present; how many more have their feet fastened to wood, not being able so much as to satisfy their bodily needs—whereas I am like a king with my legs stretched out." When I heard this, I recounted it to the brethren and they were edified.'

83. A brother asked an old man, 'If some trouble comes to me and I have no one with whom I can speak of it in confidence, what ought I to do?' The old man said, 'I think that God will send you his grace and will help you if you ask him sincerely. For truly I have heard tell that the following thing happened in Scetis: There was a good warrior monk; he did not confide in anyone, and he prepared his cloak to go away; and behold the grace of God appeared to him in the form of a virgin who encouraged him, saying, "Do not by any means go away, but remain here with me, for none of the evils of which you have spoken has happened." He was convinced and remained, and immediately his heart was healed.'

84.   A brother asked one of the Fathers if one is defiled by having evil thoughts. There was a discussion on the subject, and some said, 'Yes, one is defiled', and others, 'No, or else—poor men that we are—we could not be saved; what counts is not to carry them out corporally.' The brother went to a very experienced old man to question him about the discussion. The old man said to him, 'What is required of each one is regulated according to his capacity.' The brother begged the old man to explain, saying, 'For the Lord's sake, explain this saying.' The old man said to him, 'Suppose a tempting object is placed here and two brothers, of whom one is more advanced in virtue than the other, come in. He who is perfect says to himself, "I should very much like to have this object", but he does not rest in this thought; he cuts it off at once and he is not defiled; but if he who has not yet come to this measure desires the object and his thought clings to it—still if he does not take it—he also is not defiled.'

85.   An old man used to tell how one day someone committed a serious sin. Filled with compunction, he went to confess it to an old man; but he did not say what he had done, simply, 'If a thought of this kind comes upon someone, can he be saved?' And the old man, who was without experience of discernment, said to him, 'He has lost his soul'. When he heard this, the brother said to himself, 'If I am lost, I may as well return to the world.' As he was returning, he decided to go and manifest his thoughts to Abba Sylvain. Now this Abba Sylvain possessed great spiritual discernment. Coming up to him, the brother did not say what he had done, but proceeded in the same way, 'If thoughts of this kind come upon someone, can he be saved?' The father opened his mouth and beginning with the Scriptures, he attempted to show him that condemnation is not the lot of those who have these thoughts. When he heard this, the brother's hope revived, and he also told him what he had done. Like a good doctor, the father, with the help of the Scriptures, tended his soul, showing him that repentance is possible for those who seriously turn to God. Later on, our abba went to visit the other father, related all this to him, and said, 'Look how he who despaired of himself and was on the point of returning to the world has become like a star in the midst of the brethren.' I have related this so that we may know what danger there is in manifestation, whether of thoughts or of sins, to those who do not have discernment.

86.   An old man said, 'What condemns us is not that thoughts enter into us but that we use them badly; indeed, through our thoughts we can be shipwrecked, and through our thoughts we can be crowned.'

87.   A brother asked an old man, 'What shall I do, for the temptations which war against me are many, and I do not know how to fight against them?' The old man said to him, 'Do not fight against all of them, but against one only, for all a monk's temptations have one single head. So it is against this head that one must be on guard and fight, and thus all temptations diminish.'

88.   Concerning evil thoughts, the same old man replied, 'My brothers, I beseech you, just as we have cut off deeds, so let us cut off desires also.'

89.   An old man said, 'He who wishes to dwell in the desert must be capable of teaching and not need to be taught, or he will suffer harm.'

90.   An old man was asked, 'How can I find God?' He said, 'In fasting, in watching, in labours, in devotion, and, above all, in discernment. I tell you, many have injured their bodies without discernment and have gone away from us having achieved nothing. Our mouths smell bad through fasting, we know the Scriptures by heart, we recite all the Psalms of David, but we have not that which God seeks: charity and humility.'

91.   A brother said to an old man, 'Abba, I go and beg the old men to speak to me about the salvation of my soul, and I do not remember any of their words, so what ought I to do? Continue to ask them, but do nothing? In truth, I am altogether in impurity.' Now there were two empty jugs there, and the old man said to him, 'Bring me one of the jugs, put oil in it and wash it, then go and put it back in its place.' He did this several times. The old man said to him, 'Now bring the two jugs together, and see which is the cleaner.' The brother said, 'That in which I put the oil.' The old man said to him, 'So it is also for the soul; for, even if it retains nothing of what it has asked, yet it is more purified than the one which has not asked anything.'

92.   A brother lived in the stillness of prayer. Wishing to lead him astray, the demons appeared to him looking like angels, and awoke him

for the *synaxis* and showed him a light. So he went to see an old man and said to him, 'Abba, angels come with a light and awaken me for the *synaxis*.' The old man said to him, 'Do not listen to them, my child, for they are demons, but when they come to waken you say, "I wake myself when I wish but I do not listen to you".' The brother accepted the advice from the old man and returned to his cell, and the following night the demons came again, as usual, to awaken him. But, as the old man had advised him, he replied, 'I awaken myself when I wish, and as for you, I am not listening to you.' They said to him, 'That evil old man has deceived you; indeed he is a liar, for a brother came to him to borrow a piece of money, and although he had one, he lied, saying, "I haven't any", and he did not give it him. By this know that he is a liar.' At dawn the brother went to visit the old man and informed him of all this. The old man said, 'I have a piece of money, I acknowledge it, and a brother came trying to obtain it, and I did not give it to him. In truth, I knew that if I had given it to him, our souls would have suffered harm, and I thought it was more important to break a single commandment rather than to break all ten and suffer harm. But as for you, do not listen to the demons who want to deceive you.' So he returned to his cell greatly comforted by the old man.

93.   An old man said, 'The life of the monk is obedience, meditation, not judging, not slandering, not complaining. In truth it is written, "You who love the Lord, hate evil" (Ps. 97:10). The life of the monk is: not to take of him who is unjust; not to look at what is evil; not to interfere in everything; not to listen to irrelevant words; not to steal, but rather to give; not to be puffed up in his heart; not to have thoughts of fornication; not to be greedy; to do everything with discernment. The life of the monk consists in these things.

94.   Concerning a great old man, some of the Fathers used to relate that if one came to him to ask for a word, he would say, 'Look, I am going to play the part of God and seat myself on the throne of judgment. What do you want me to do for you, then? If you say, "Have mercy on me", God says to you, "If you want me to have mercy on you, do you also have mercy on your brother; if you want me to forgive you, do you also forgive your neighbour". Can there be injustice in God? Certainly not, but it depends on us whether we wish to be saved.'

95. One of the old men of the Cells was said to give himself much hardship. Once when he was saying the *synaxis*, another of the saints came to see him, and from outside he heard him striving with his thoughts and saying, 'For the sake of a single word, how long am I going to let all the others go?' And the visitor thought he was fighting with someone, and he knocked so as to go in and reconcile them. Entering, then, and seeing there was no one else inside, since he could speak freely with the old man, he said to him, 'With whom were you striving, abba?' He said to him, 'With my thoughts. In truth I know fourteen books of the Scriptures by heart, and having heard a single paltry word, when I give myself to saying my *synaxis*, all the books vanish and this single word comes to me at the time of the *synaxis*. That is why I was fighting with my thoughts.'

96. An old man said, 'The prophets wrote books, then came our Fathers who put them into practice. Those who came after them learnt them by heart. Then came the present generation, who have written them out and put them into their window seats without using them.'

97. Some brothers from a monastery went to the desert to visit an anchorite who received them with joy. According to the custom amongst hermits, when he saw their fatigue, he set the table before the usual time and brought what he had to refresh them. When evening came, they recited the twelve Psalms, and likewise during the night. While he was keeping vigil all alone, he heard them saying amongst themselves, 'The anchorites in the desert have a softer life than we do in the monastery'. At early dawn while they were preparing to leave and to visit the neighbouring old man, he said to them, 'Greet him from me and say to him, "Do not water the vegetables".' This they did. When he heard these words, the other old man understood what it meant, and he kept them at work until evening. When evening came, he recited the great *synaxis* and said, 'Let us stop now, for your sakes, for you are tired', and he went on, 'It is not our custom to eat every day, but for your sakes let us eat a little.' He brought them dry bread and salt saying, 'For your sake we must celebrate', and he poured a little vinegar on the salt. When they rose from table, they said the *synaxis* till early dawn. Then he said to them, 'We cannot fulfil the whole rule on your account; you must take a little rest, for you come from far.' When morning came, they wanted to escape, but he begged them saying, 'Stay yet awhile with us, at least three days according to the com-

31

mandment, so as to follow the traditional custom of the desert.' But seeing that he would not send them away, they arose and escaped secretly.

98. A brother questioned one of the Fathers, saying, 'If I happen to be overcome by sleep and miss the proper time for the *synaxis*, I am afraid of what people will think and I no longer want to say the prayers late.' The old man said to him, 'If it happens that you are drowsy till morning, get up, shut your door and your window, and say the *synaxis*. For truly it is written, "The day is yours and the night is yours also." (Ps. 74:61.) In truth, God is glorified at all times.'

99. An old man said, 'There was a man who ate a lot and was still hungry, and another who ate little and was satisfied. The one who ate a lot and was still hungry received a greater reward than he who ate little and was satisfied.'

100. An old man said, 'If an unpleasant word is spoken between you and someone else, and the other denies it saying, 'I did not say that word', do not enter into argument with him saying, 'You did say it', for he will begin to retort, 'Yes, I did say it, and what if I did?'

101. A brother asked an old man, 'My sister is poor. If I am charitable towards her is it not the same as if I were charitable to another poor person?' The old man said, 'No.' The brother said, 'Why, abba?' The old man said, 'Because blood is thicker than water.'

102. An old man said, 'Do not agree with every word. Be slow to believe, quick to speak the truth.'

103. An old man said, 'Even though the saints suffer here below, yet have they in part already received rest.' He said this because they were set free from all worldly cares.

104. An old man said, 'If a monk knows a place where he can make progress, but where he can get the necessities of life only with difficulty, and for that reason he does not go there, such a monk does not believe that God exists.'

105. A brother questioned a young monk, saying, 'Is it better to be silent or to speak?' The young man said to him, 'If the words are useless, leave them alone, but if they are good, give place to the good and speak. Furthermore, even if they are good, do not prolong speech, but terminate it quickly, and you will have peace, quiet, rest.'

106. One of the old men said, 'In the beginning, when we came together, we spoke to the good of souls, we advanced and ascended to heaven; now when we come together we fall into slander, and we drag one another to hell.'

107. One of the Fathers said, 'If the interior man is watchful, he can preserve the exterior man also; if this is not the case, let us guard our tongue as much as we can.'

108. The same old man said, 'Spiritual work is essential, it is for this we have come to the desert. It is very hard to teach with the mouth that which one does not practise in the body.

109. One of the Fathers said, 'A man should always have an interior occupation. If he gives himself to the work of God, the enemy who approaches him from time to time will not find a dwelling place in him. On the other hand, if he is dominated by the captivity of the enemy, though the Spirit of God often presents himself, because he does not allow him room, he withdraws because of his evil ways.'

110. One day some monks went down from Egypt to Scetis to visit the old men. They noticed that the hunger caused by their *ascesis* made them eat ravenously, and they were shocked. When the priest learned this, he wanted to correct them. He made the following proclamation to the people in church: 'My brothers, fast, and intensify your *ascesis*.' When the Egyptian visitors wanted to go away he held them back. After the first day of fasting they were tired. But he made them eat every other day, while the monks of Scetis fasted the whole week. When Saturday came, the Egyptians sat down to eat with the old men. Now the Egyptians ate voraciously, so one of the old men took them by the hand, saying, 'Eat with moderation, like monks.' But one of them pushed his hand away, saying, 'Let me alone, for I am starving not having eaten anything cooked

the whole week'. The old man said, 'If you, who have eaten every other day, are so exhausted, how could you be shocked at brothers who always follow an *ascesis* like this?' Then the Egyptians asked forgiveness of the monks of Scetis and went away joyfully, greatly edified.

111. A brother who had withdrawn and taken the habit shut himself up immediately, saying, 'I am an anchorite'. When they heard him say this, the old men came to drive him away and made him go the round of all the brethren's cells, bowing before them and saying, 'Forgive me, for I am not an anchorite, but a beginner'.

112. The old men used to say, 'When you see a young man ascending up to heaven through his own will, seize him by the foot and pull him down, for this is good for him.'

113. A brother said to a great old man, 'Abba, I want to find an old man to my liking and die with him.' And the old man said to him, 'My lord, much good may your search do you!' But the brother was profoundly convinced that it really was good, and did not ponder the old man's saying. When the old man saw that he thought he was really looking for something good, he said to him, 'If you find an old man after your own mind, will you stay with him?' The other said, 'Yes, altogether, if I find him to my liking.' The old man said to him, 'Perhaps it is not that you will follow the old man's will, but that he will follow yours, that will give you peace?' Then the brother arose, realizing what he had said, bowed before him and said, 'Forgive me, I was conceited thinking I had said something good when it was actually nothing'.

114. Two brothers according to the flesh withdrew from the world. The first to take the habit was the younger. When one of the Fathers came to visit them they brought a basin and the younger came to wash his feet, but seizing him by the hand the old man prevented him and put the elder in his place. The old men who were present said to him, 'Abba, the younger was the first to take the habit.' The old man said to them, 'But I take away the primacy from the younger and transfer it to the elder.'

115. An old man said, 'If someone lives in a place and does not reap the fruit which that place affords, it will drive him away because he has not known how to work there.'

116. An old man said, 'If someone acts according to his own will and not according to God—but does it in ignorance—he must afterwards come into the way of God. But he who is attached to his own will and does not act according to God and refuses to listen to others, but believes he knows what is right, such a man reaches the way of God only with difficulty.'

117. An old man was asked, 'What is the straight and narrow way?' He replied, 'The straight way is this, to do violence to one's thoughts and to cut off one's own will. That is what this means: "Behold we have left all and followed Thee".' (Mark 10:28.)

118. An old man said, 'Just as the monastic state is regarded more highly than the secular state, so should the visiting monk be in all ways a mirror for the monks of the place he visits.'

119. One of the Fathers said, 'If a hard-working monk lives in a place where there are no other hard-working monks, he cannot make progress: he can only struggle so as not to get worse; but if a lazy monk dwells with hard-working monks, he makes progress if he is vigilant, and if not he does not get any worse.'

120. An old man said, 'If the soul has the word but not the work, it is like a tree with leaves but no fruit. But just as a tree full of fruit also has beautiful foliage, so words are appropriate in the soul whose activity is good.'

121. An old man said, 'Do not do anything you hate to another. You do not like it when someone slanders you? Then do not slander anyone. You do not like it if someone denounces you falsely? Then do not denounce anybody. You do not like it if someone despises you, injures you, or steals something from you? Then do nothing of this sort to another. He who can keep this saying has what he needs for salvation.'

THAT ONE MUST BE WATCHFUL NOT TO JUDGE ANYONE

122. A provincial priest went to visit an anchorite to offer the Eucharist for him. Now someone went to the anchorite and spoke against the priest, so when the latter came according to custom to give him com-

munion, the anchorite, who had been shocked, did not let him in, and the priest went away. Then, behold, a voice came to the anchorite, saying, 'Men have taken my judgment away from me.' The anchorite was as though in ecstasy, and he saw a well of gold and a rope of gold and a jug of gold and much water of surpassing quality. Then he saw a leper draw the water and pour it out, and he would gladly have drunk but could not because he who drew the water was leprous. Again a voice came to him saying, 'Why do you not drink the water? What does it matter if he who draws it is leprous? He only draws it and pours it out.' Returning to himself and perceiving the meaning of the vision, the anchorite sent for the priest and let him give him communion as usual.

123. In a monastery there were two remarkable brothers who soon merited to see the grace of God descend upon each other. Now one day it happened that one of them went out of the monastery on a Friday and saw someone who was eating in the morning, and he said to him, 'Why are you eating at this hour on a Friday?' Later there was the *synaxis* as usual. Now his brother saw that grace had withdrawn from him, and he was grieved. When they had returned to the cell he said to him, 'My brother, what have you done? Indeed, I do not see the grace of God upon you as it used to be.' The other answered him, 'I am not aware of having done anything wrong, either in act or in thought.' His brother said to him, 'Have you spoken any words?' Then he remembered and said, 'Yesterday I saw someone who was eating outside the monastery early in the day, and I said to him, "Why are you eating at this hour on a Friday?" This is my sin. But labour with me for two weeks, praying God to forgive me.' They did this, and at the end of two weeks one brother saw the grace of God come upon the other and they were comforted and gave thanks to God.

THAT ONE SHOULD DO NOTHING WITH OSTENTATION
AND THAT ONE SHOULD SHUN AMBITION

124. One day there was a festival at the Cells, and the brethren were eating in church. Now there was there a brother who said to the servant, 'I do not eat anything cooked, but only with salt. He who was serving said in a loud voice to another brother before everyone, 'Brother so and so eats nothing cooked, bring him some salt.' Then one of the old men got up and

said to him, 'It would have been better for you to have eaten meat in your cell than to hear this said about you in front of everyone.'

125. An ascetic brother who did not eat bread went to visit a great old man. Now some other visitors were there, and for their sake the old man had done a little cooking. They sat down to eat, and the ascetic put only a few soaked peas in front of him and ate them. When they arose from table, the old man took him aside and said to him, 'Brother, when you go to visit someone, do not let your way of life be seen. But if you want to hold to your *ascesis*, remain in your cell and never come out of it.' Taught by this saying of the old man's, he learnt to do as everyone else when he was with the brethren.

126. Someone begged an old man to accept some money for his needs, but he refused, saying that his manual work supplied all that was necessary. When the other insisted that he should accept at least enough for his essential needs, the old man replied, 'It would be a double shame to accept it: for me to receive what I do not need, and for you to give me what belongs to others.'

127. An important person came from abroad to Scetis bringing much gold with him, and he asked the priest to give some of it to the brothers. The priest said, 'The brothers do not need it', but as the other was very insistent, he put a basket filled with gold at the door of the church. The priest said, 'Let anyone who needs it take some.' But nobody came, and some did not even notice it was there. So the priest said to the visitor, 'God has seen your charity; go, and give it to the poor.' Greatly edified, the man went away.

128. Someone brought some money to an old man saying, 'Keep it for your expenses, for you are getting old and you are ill.' The old man was indeed infirm, but he replied, 'Are you really going to take my prize from me after sixty years, for I have been ill as long as that? I need nothing. God supplies what I need and feeds me.' So he refused to take the money.

129. The old men used to tell of a gardener who worked and gave away all his labours in charity keeping only what he needed for himself. Later on, Satan suggested this to him: 'Put a little money aside for when

you are old or sick and have expenses to pay.' He put money aside and filled a purse. Now he fell ill and one of his feet became gangrenous. And he spent all the money on doctors without getting any help from it. Later on, an experienced doctor came and said to him, 'If your foot is not cut off, your whole body will become gangrenous.' So he decided to have his foot cut off. The same night, coming to his senses, and repenting of what he had done, he began to groan and to weep, saying, 'Lord, remember my former works when I used to labour and to give to the brethren', and while he was saying this an angel of the Lord came and said to him, 'Where is the purse you collected? What did you hope to gain from it?' Then he pondered and said, 'Lord, I have sinned. Forgive me; henceforth I will do it no more.' Then the angel touched his foot and it was healed immediately. In the early dawn he got up and went to work in the fields. The doctor came as arranged, with his instruments to cut off the foot, and not finding him he asked his neighbour where the sick man was. The other said to him, 'In the morning he went to work in the fields.' Surprised, the doctor went to the fields where he was working and seeing him digging, he glorified God who had healed him.

130. A brother asked an old man, 'Will you let me put two pieces of money aside in case I should be ill?' The old man replied, 'It is not good to keep more than is necessary for the body. If you keep these two pieces of money your hope will be placed in them, and if misfortune comes to you God will no longer look after you.' Let us throw all our care on God, for he cares for us.

131. Some pagans came to Ostrakina to give alms there, and they took the stewards with them to show them the people who were most in need. The stewards took them to see a mutilated man, and they offered him alms, but he, refusing to accept it, said, 'I work by plaiting reed branches, and I eat my bread'. Then the stewards took them to the cell of a widow living with her child. They knocked on the door, and the girl, who was naked, replied to them from behind the door that her mother had gone to work (for she was a laundress). They supplied her with a garment and some money, but she did not want to accept them, saying, 'My mother came, telling me to have confidence for God has indeed willed that she should find work today and that we should have some food.' When her mother came, the visitors begged her to accept it, but she refused it,

saying, 'I have God who cares for me, and would you really deprive me of that?' When they heard of such faith, they gave glory to God.

THAT ONE MUST ALWAYS BE VIGILANT

132. An old man said, 'Every evening and every morning a monk ought to render an account of himself and say to himself, "What have we not done of what God does not want, and what have we done of that which God wills?" In this way he must live in repentance. This is what it means to be a monk, and this is how Abba Arsenius used to live.'

133. An old man said, 'He who loses gold or silver can find more to replace it, but he who loses time cannot find more.'

134. One of the old men went to another old man one day, and while they were speaking, the first said, 'I am dead to the world'. The other old man said, 'Do not count on it, brother, before you have left the body, for even if you say you are dead, yet Satan is not dead.'

135. An old man said, 'Just as the soldier and the hunter when they go to fight are not concerned about knowing whether others are wounded or saved, but each one fights on his own account, so must the monk be.'

136. An old man said, 'Just as no one can cause harm to someone who is close to the king, no more can Satan do anything to us if our souls are close to God, for truly he said, "Draw near to me, and I shall be near to you". But since we often exalt ourselves, the enemy has no difficulty in drawing our poor souls into shameful passions.'

137. An old man said, 'Having arisen in the early hours, say to yourself, "Body, you must work to feed yourself; soul, be vigilant in order to receive the inheritance".'

138. A brother said to an old man, 'I do not see any warfare in my heart.' The old man said to him, 'Then you are a building open on all four sides; whoever wishes to goes in and out of you, but you do not notice it. But if you had a door and shut it and did not let the evil thoughts come in through it, then you would see them standing outside warring against you.'

139. It was said of an old man that when his thoughts said to him, 'Relax today, and tomorrow repent', he retorted, 'No, I am going to repent today, and may the will of God be done tomorrow'.

140. An old man said, 'If the inner man is not vigilant it is not possible to guard the outer man.'

141. The old men used to say, 'The powers of Satan which go before all sin are three: forgetfulness, negligence, and desire. For, truly, every time forgetfulness comes, it engenders negligence; and from negligence, desire proceeds; and desire causes a man to fall. But if the spirit stands on guard against Satan, it does not give way to desire; if it does not desire, by the grace of Christ it does not fall.'

142. An old man said, 'Practise silence, be careful for nothing, give heed to your meditation, lie down and get up in the fear of God, and you will not need to fear the assaults of the impious.'

143. An old man said to a brother, 'The devil is the enemy and you yourself are the house. The enemy never stops throwing all that he finds into your house, pouring all sorts of impurities over it. It is your part not to neglect throwing them outside again. If you do not do this the house will be filled with all sorts of impurities and you will no longer be able to get inside. But all that the other begins to throw in, you should throw out again little by little, and by the grace of Christ your house will remain pure.'

144. One of the old men said, 'When the eyes of the ox are covered he turns the mill, but if they are not covered he does not turn it. Even so does the devil. If he succeeds in covering a man's eyes he weakens him and leads him to commit all kinds of sin, but if a man's eyes are full of light it is easy for him to flee from the devil.'

145. They used to say that seven monks lived on Abba Antony's mountain. At the time of palm harvest, one of them had to keep guard to drive away the birds. Now there was an old man there, and when it was his day to watch he began to cry out, 'Go away you bad thoughts inside and you birds outside.'

146. A brother at the Cells soaked his palm leaves, and when he sat down to weave them his thoughts said to him, 'Go and visit such and such an old man'. Then he thought within himself, 'I will go in a few days'. His thoughts said to him again, 'And if he dies, what will you do? Go and speak to him because it is the right time.' He said again within himself, 'But this is not the moment'. His thoughts suggested to him, 'But when you have cut the reeds it will be the right moment', so he said, 'I am going to finish the palms and then I will go'. Then he said within himself, 'However, the air is good today', and he got up, left his palm leaves soaking, took his sheepskin, and went out. Now his neighbour there was an old man who had the gift of vision. When he saw him running, he called out, 'Prisoner, prisoner, come here'. When he came, the old man said to him, 'Go back to your cell'. Then the brother told him about his struggle, and when he got back to his cell again he bowed down in penitence. Then the demons cried out in a loud voice, 'O monks, you have overcome us.' The mat on which he was sitting was burnt as by fire, while the demons became invisible like smoke.

147. They used to tell of an old man who was dying at Scetis. His brethren were standing round his bed putting the habit on him and weeping, but he opened his eyes and laughed; then he laughed a second and a third time. The brothers asked him, 'Abba, tell us how it is that while we are weeping you laugh.' He said to them, 'I laughed because you all fear death; I laughed a second time because you are not ready; and I laughed a third time because I am leaving labour for rest.' And immediately the old man fell asleep.

148. Some brothers narrated the following story: 'One day we went to visit the old men and as was customary, once we had said the prayers and they had greeted us, we sat down. After talking with them we wanted to leave, and we asked them to say a prayer. One of the old men said, "What do you mean? Have you not been praying?" We said, "Abba, there was the prayer when we came, but up till now we have been talking." The old man said, "Forgive me, brothers, but there is a brother sitting with you and talking who has said three hundred prayers." When he had said that, they said the prayer, and took leave of us.'

C

149. An old man and a brother led their life together. Now the old man was charitable. It happened that there was a famine and people came to his door seeking alms, and in charity the old man gave to all who came. Seeing what was happening, the brother said to the old man, 'Give me my share of the loaves, and do what you like with yours.' The old man divided the loaves and gave alms from his share. Now many people hastened to the old man, learning that he supplied everyone, and God—seeing that he supplied everyone—blessed these loaves. But when the brother had consumed his own food he said to the old man, 'Since I have only a little food left, abba, take me back into the common life again.' The old man said, 'I will do as you wish.' So they began again to live in common. When scarcity came again, the needy came back seeking alms. Now one day the brother came in and saw they were short of loaves. A poor man came, and the old man told the brother to give him alms. He said, 'It is no longer possible, father.' The old man said to him, 'Go in and look.' The brother went inside and found the bin full of loaves. When he saw that, he was filled with fear, and taking some he gave to the poor. In this way he learned the faith and virtue of the old man, and he gave glory to God.

150. An old man said, 'There are monks who do many good works, and the evil one sends them scruples about quite little things, to cause them to lose the fruit of the good they have done. When I happened to be living in Oxyrhynchus near a priest who gave alms to many, a widow came to ask him for some wheat. He said to her, "Bring a sack and I will measure some out for you." She brought it, and measuring the sack with his hand, he said, "It is a big sack." Now this filled the widow with shame. I said to him, "Abba, have you sold the wheat?" He said, "No, I gave it her in charity." I said to him, "If you gave it all to her in alms, why did you cavil at the amount and fill her with shame?" '

151. A brother went to see an anchorite and as he was leaving said to him, 'Forgive me, abba, for having taken you away from your rule.' But the other answered him, 'My rule is to refresh you and send you away in peace.'

152. An anchorite was living close to a monastery, and he led a very austere life. Now it happened that some visitors came to the monastery and constrained him to eat outside the proper time. Afterwards the brothers said to him, 'Abba, were you not grieved by that?' He said to them, 'I am grieved only when I do my own will.'

153. It was said of an old man that he dwelt in Syria on the way to the desert. This was his work: whenever a monk came from the desert he gave him refreshment with all his heart. Now one day an anchorite came, to whom he gave refreshment, but the other did not want to accept it, saying he was fasting. Filled with sorrow, the old man said to him, 'Do not disregard your servant, I beg you; do not despise me, but let us pray. Look at the tree which is here—we will follow the way of whichever of us causes it to bend when he kneels on the ground and prays.' So the anchorite knelt down to pray, and nothing happened. Then the hospitable one knelt down, and at once the tree bent towards him. Taught by this, they gave thanks to God.

154. A monk had a brother living in the world who was poor, and so he supplied him with all he received from his work. But the more the monk supplied, the poorer the brother became. So the monk went to tell an old man about it. The old man said to him, 'If you want my advice, do not give him anything more, but say to him, "Brother, when I had something I supplied you; now bring me what you get from your work." Take all he brings you, and whenever you see a stranger or a poor man, give him some of it, begging him to pray for him.' The monk went away and did this. When his secular brother came, he spoke to him as the old man had said, and the brother went sadly away. The first day, taking some vegetables from his field, he brought them to the monk. The monk took them and gave them to the old men, begging them to pray for his brother, and after the blessing he returned home. In the same way, another time, the brother brought the monk some vegetables and three loaves, which he took, doing as on the first occasion, and having received the blessing he went away. And the secular brother came a third time bringing many provisions, some bread, and fish. Seeing this, the monk was full of wonder, and he invited the poor so as to give them refreshment. Then he said to his brother, 'Do you not need a little bread?' The other said to him, 'No, for when I used to receive something from you, it was like a fire coming into

my house and burning it, but now that I receive nothing from you, God blesses me.' Then the monk went to tell the old man all that had happened, and the old man said to him, 'Do you not know that the work of the monk is of fire, and where it enters, it burns? It helps your brother more to do alms with what he reaps from his field, and to receive the prayers of the saints and thus to be blessed.'

155. A monk of the Thebaid had received the charism of service from God so that he was able to provide all who came to him with what they needed. Now he happened to be giving alms one day in a village, and a woman wearing old clothes came towards him to receive something. Seeing that she was wearing old clothes, he opened his hand to give her a lot, but his hand closed, and he paid out little. Then a woman came to him wearing good clothes. Seeing her clothes, he sought to give her little, but his hand opened, and he gave away much. So he enquired concerning the two women, and they told him, 'The one wearing good clothes belongs to the leading classes, and she has become poor; in memory of this she wears good clothes. But the other one wears old clothes so as to receive more.'

156. Two brothers went to see an old man one day. Now it was not the old man's custom to eat every day. When he saw the brothers he rejoiced and said, 'Fasting brings its reward, but he who eats through charity fulfils two precepts, for he gives up his own will and he fulfils the commandment of charity.' And he gave the brothers refreshment.

157. There was a saint in Egypt who dwelt in a desert place. Far away from him there was a Manichean who was a priest (at least what they call a priest). Once, when this man was going to visit one of his confederates, night overtook him in the place where the orthodox saint was living. He was in great distress, fearing to go to him to sleep there, for he knew that he was known as a Manichean, and he was afraid he would not be received. However, finding himself compelled to do so, he knocked; and the old man opened the door to him, recognized him, received him joyfully, constrained him to pray, and after having given him refreshment, he made him sleep. Thinking this over during the night, the Manichean said, 'How is it that he is without any suspicions about me? Truly, this man is of God.' And he threw himself at his feet, saying, 'Henceforth, I am orthodox', and he stayed with him.

158. The old men used to say, 'If someone has faith in another, and hands himself over to him in complete submission, he does not need to pay attention to God's commands but he can entrust his whole will to his father. He will suffer no reproach from God, for God looks for nothing from beginners so much as renunciation through obedience.'

159. A brother at Scetis was preparing to go to the harvest and he went to see an old man and said to him, 'Tell me what I should do when I go harvesting.' The old man said to him, 'If I tell you, will you believe me?' The brother said, 'Yes, I am listening to you.' The old man said to him, 'If you trust me, go and give up this harvesting, come here and I will tell you what to do.' So the brother gave up harvesting and came to live with the old man. The old man said to him, 'Go into your cell, spend fifty days eating dry bread and salt only once a day, and come back and I will tell you what else to do.' The brother went away, did this, then came back to the old man. The old man, seeing that he was a worker, taught him how to live in the cell. The brother went away to his cell and prostrated himself to the ground, weeping before God. After this, when his thoughts said to him, 'You are trained, you have become a great man', he placed his sins before his eyes, saying, 'And where are all my omissions?' But when his thoughts in the opposite sense said to him, 'You have committed many sins', he in his turn replied, 'Yet I say my few prayers to God, and I trust that God will have mercy on me.' Being overcome, the evil spirits appeared to him openly saying, 'We have been disturbed by you.' He asked them why. They said to him, 'When we exalt you, you run to humility; but when we humiliate you, then you rise up.'

160. An old man had a servant who lived in the village. Now it once happened that when the servant delayed to come according to custom the old man was without what he needed, and when his delay was protracted, he lacked even what he needed for his work in his cell. Vexed at not having what he needed, either for working or for eating, he said to his disciple, 'Will you go to the village?' The latter said, 'I will do as you wish.' Now the brother feared to go into the village on account of scandal, but he agreed to go so as not to disobey his father. The old man said to him, 'Go, and I trust that the God of my Fathers will protect you from all

temptation', and saying the prayer, he sent him away.

When he got to the village, the brother asked where the servant dwelt, and he found out. Now it happened that the servant and all his household were out of the village at the cemetery, except for one of his daughters who answered the disciple when he knocked on the door. When she had opened the door from inside and seen him, he asked her about her father, but she invited him to come inside, and even drew him in, but he refused. When she persisted for a long time, she ended by drawing him to herself, but seeing himself forced towards impurity, and feeling that he was going to consent to his desires, he prayed with groans to God, saying, 'Lord, by the prayers of my father, save me in this hour.' At these words he immediately found himself on the river, returning to the monastery, and he returned unharmed to his father.

161. Two brothers by blood went to live in a monastery. One was an ascetic and the other was very obedient. When the father told him to do this or that, he would do it; if to eat in the morning, he would eat. He was highly thought of in the monastery because of his obedience. His brother, the ascetic, was acutely annoyed at this and said to himself, 'I am going to test him to see if he really possesses obedience.' So he went to the father and said, 'Send my brother with me so that we can go somewhere.' The father told him to go, and the ascetic took him with the intention of putting him to the test. They went to the river. Now there were many crocodiles there, and he said to him, 'Go down to the river and cross.' He went down, and the crocodiles came to lick his body, but they did him no harm. Seeing this, the ascetic said, 'Come up from the river.' As they went on their way they found a corpse thrown on the side of the road. The ascetic said, 'If we had some old rags we could throw them over him', but he who was obedient said, 'Let us rather pray that he may come to life again.' They began to pray, and during their prayer the dead man came to life again. The ascetic was puffed up, saying, 'It is because of my asceticism that the dead man has come to life again.' But God revealed everything to the father of the monastery and how the ascetic had put his brother to the test with the crocodiles and how the dead man had come to life. When they came to the monastery the abba said to the ascetic, 'What have you done to your brother? It is because of his obedience that the dead man came to life again.

162. A brother who lived in the world had three children. He withdrew to a monastery, leaving them in the city. After spending three years in the monastery, his thoughts began to remind him of his children, and he was very uneasy about them. Now he had not told the abba that he had children. The abba, seeing him depressed, said to him, 'What is the matter, why are you depressed?' He told the abba that he had three children in the city and he wanted to bring them to the monastery. The abba ordered him to do so. Going to the city, he found the first two were dead, and he took back the remaining one. He came to the monastery and looking for the abba, he found him in the bakery. Seeing him, the abba greeted him, and taking the child in his arms he covered him with kisses, saying to the child's father, 'Do you love him?' The other said that he did. 'Do you love him very much?' He answered, 'Yes.' Hearing this, the abba said, 'Take him and throw him into the furnace so that it burns him', so the father took his own child and threw him into the furnace which immediately became like dew, full of freshness. Through this act he received glory like the patriarch Abraham.

163. An old man said, 'He who lives in obedience to a spiritual father finds more profit in it than one who withdraws to the desert.'

164. An old man said, 'The reason why we do not make progress is because we do not know our own measure, and we do not persevere in the work we undertake, and we want to acquire virtue without labour.'

OF HUMILITY

165. A man possessed by the devil, who was foaming terribly at the mouth, struck a hermit-monk on the cheek. The old man turned and offered him the other. Then the devil, unable to bear the burning of humility, disappeared immediately.

166. An old man said, 'Every time a thought of superiority or vanity moves you, examine your conscience to see if you have kept all the commandments, if you love your enemies and are grieved at their sins, if you consider yourself as an unprofitable servant and the greatest sinner of all. Even then, do not pretend to great ideas as though you were perfectly right, for this thought destroys everything.

167. An old man said, 'He who is honoured and praised more than he deserves suffers great harm thereby; whereas one who is not honoured by men at all will be glorified above.'

168. A brother asked an old man, 'Is it good to make many prostrations?' The old man said, 'We see that God appeared to Joshua, son of Nun, when he was prostrate.' (Jos. 5:14.)

169. An old man was asked, 'Why are we thus warred against by the demons?' He said, 'Because we have cast away our arms; I mean, contempt of honours, humility, poverty, and endurance.'

170. A brother asked an old man, 'If a brother tells me irrelevant things, do you advise me, abba, to ask him not to do so?' The old man said he did not. Then the brother asked why, and the old man said, 'Because we are not able to do this ourselves, and for fear lest having asked our neighbour not to do it, we later find that we are doing it.' The brother said, 'So what should one do?' The old man said, 'If we wish to keep silence, this way of doing it is enough for our neighbour.'

171. An old man was asked, 'What is humility?' He replied, 'It is when your brother sins against you and you forgive him before he comes to ask for forgiveness.'

172. An old man said, 'In all trials do not blame others but only yourself, saying, "It is because of my sins that this has happened." '

173. A brother questioned an old man, saying, 'What is humility?' And the old man said, 'To do good to one who does evil to you.' The brother said, 'And if you do not reach this standard?' The old man said, 'You must go away and choose to be silent.'

174. A brother asked an old man, 'What is the work of one who lives as an exile?' The old man said, 'I used to know a brother who was living in exile and then happened to go to church. By chance there was an *agape* and the brother sat down to eat with the other brethren, and some amongst them said, "Now who has invited this man?" So they said to him, "Get up and go away", and he got up and went away. Some of the others

were grieved at this and they went to call him back. Afterwards they asked him, "What was in your heart when you were driven away and then brought back again?" He said, "I was quite sure in my heart that I was like a dog. When it is driven away, it goes, and when it is called, it comes." '

175. Some visitors came to the Thebaid one day to visit an old man, bringing one possessed with a devil that he might heal him. When they persistently asked him, the old man said to the devil, 'Come out of God's creature.' And the devil said to the old man, 'I am going to come out, but I am going to ask you a question, tell me, who are the goats and who are the sheep?' The old man said, 'I am one of the goats, but as for the sheep, God alone knows who they are.' When he heard this the devil began to cry out with a loud voice, 'Because of your humility, I am going away', and he departed at the same hour.

176. An Egyptian monk was living in a suburb of Constantinople at the time of the Emperor Theodosius the Younger. As he was passing by this way, the Emperor left his suite and came alone to knock on the monk's door. The latter opened the door and knew very well who it was, but he welcomed him like an officer. When he had come in, they said a prayer and sat down. The Emperor began to ask him, 'How are the Fathers in Egypt?' The monk said, 'They are all praying for your salvation', and he said to him, 'Eat a little'. He soaked some loaves and added a little oil and some salt. The old man ate, and he offered the Emperor water, and he drank. Then the Emperor said to him, 'Do you know who I am?' He said, 'God knows you.' Then he said, 'I am Theodosius the Emperor.' Immediately the old man made a prostration. The Emperor said to him, 'Happy are you, for you do not have the cares of life. I was born in a palace and yet I have never enjoyed bread and water as I have today; I have eaten very well.' Henceforward the Emperor began to honour the old man, so he arose and fled again to Egypt.

177. The old men used to say, 'When we do not experience warfare, we ought so much the more to humiliate ourselves. For God, seeing our weakness, protects us; when we glorify ourselves, he withdraws his protection and we are lost.

178. The devil appeared to a brother disguised as an angel of light and said to him, 'I am Gabriel and I have been sent to you.' The brother said to him, 'See if it is not someone else to whom you have been sent; as for me, I am not worthy of it'—and immediately the devil vanished.

179. The old men used to say, 'Even if an angel should indeed appear to you, do not receive him but humiliate yourself, saying, 'I am not worthy to see an angel, for I am a sinner.'

180. It was said of an old man that while he was sitting in the cell and striving, he saw the demons visibly and he scorned them. The devil, seeing himself overcome, came to show himself to him, saying, 'I, indeed, am Christ.' When he saw him, the old man closed his eyes, and the devil said to him, 'Why do you close your eyes? I am Christ', and the old man answered him, 'I do not want to see Christ here below'. When he heard these words, the devil vanished.

181. The demons said to another old man, 'Do you want to see Christ?' He said to them, 'A curse on you and on whatever you say! In truth, I believe in my Christ who has said, "If someone says to you, here is Christ, or there he is, do not believe him".' And immediately they vanished.

182. It was said of an old man that for seventy years he ate only once a week. He asked God about the interpretation of a saying of Scripture, and God did not reveal it to him. He said to himself, 'I have given myself so much affliction without obtaining anything, so I will go to see my brother and ask him.' But while he was closing the door behind him to go to see his brother, an angel of the Lord was sent to him who said, 'These seventy years you have fasted have not brought you near to God, but when you humiliated yourself by going to see your brother, I was sent to tell you the meaning of this saying.' When he had fully replied to his search into the Scriptures he withdrew from him.

183. An old man said, 'If someone, with the fear of God and in humility, orders a brother to do something, his word, uttered for the sake of God, causes the brother to submit and fulfil what was ordered. But if someone wishes to command a brother, not according to the fear of God

but to subject him to his own authoritarian power, God, who sees the secrets of the heart, will not move the brother to listen and to fulfil it. The work which is done for God's sake is evident; that which is done through authoritarianism is also evident. The work of God is humble and it cheers; that which proceeds from authoritarianism is full of agitation and trouble, for it proceeds from evil.'

184. An old man said, 'I would rather have a defeat with humility than a victory with pride.'

185. An old man said, 'Do not despise him who stands beside you, for you do not know if the Spirit of God is on you or on him. When I say, he who stands beside you, I mean he who serves you.'

186. A brother asked an old man, 'If I am living with some brethren and see something contrary to what is right, do you want me to say so?' The old man said, 'If there are some who are older than you, or the same age as yourself, be silent and you will have peace, for in so doing you make yourself inferior to the others and you will stay free from care.' The brother said to him, 'What shall I do, father, for the spirits trouble me?' The old man said to him, 'If you suffer, tell the brothers of it once, with humility, and if they do not listen, leave your pain before God and he himself will give you peace. For to throw oneself before God signifies this: to give up one's own will. Be careful that your concern is according to God. As I see it, it is better to keep silence, for this is humility.'

187. A brother was vexed with another brother who, when he learned of it, came to ask pardon, but he did not open the door to him. So the other went to an old man and told him of the matter, and the old man replied, 'See if there is not a motive in your heart, such as blaming your brother, or thinking it is he who is responsible. You want to justify yourself, and that is why he is not moved to open the door to you. In addition I tell you this, even if it is he who has sinned against you, go, settle it in your heart that it is you who have sinned against him and think your brother is right, then God will move him to reconcile himself with you.' Convinced, the brother did thus; then he went to knock at the brother's door and almost before he heard the sound the other was first to ask pardon from inside. Then he opened the door and embraced him with all his heart. So there was deep peace between them.

188. An old man said, 'Either you should flee from all men in reality, or you are ridiculing the world and men by making yourself in all things a fool.'

189. An old man said, 'If you say to someone, "Forgive me", in humiliating yourself you are burning the demons.'

190. An old man said, 'If you acquire silence do not consider yourself as having gained a virtue, but say, "I am unworthy to speak".'

191. An old man said, 'If the baker does not put blinkers on the beast of burden, she does not turn the mill and eats his wages; so it is with us. By the divine economy we receive blinkers which prevent us from seeing the good we do, from glorifying ourselves and thus losing our reward. For this reason we are sometimes handed over to bad thoughts, and we see ourselves in order to blame ourselves. These bad thoughts become blinkers for us which hide from us the little good we do. In truth, every time a man blames himself, he does not lose his reward.'

192. Someone asked an old man, 'What is humility?' He replied, 'Humility is a great and divine work. The road leading to humility is through bodily labours, and considering oneself a sinner, inferior to all.' Then the brother said, 'What does that mean, "inferior to all"?' The old man said, 'It is this: not paying attention to others' sins, but always to one's own, praying to God ceaselessly.'

193. A brother questioned an old man, 'Tell me something which I can do, so that I may live by it', and the old man said, 'If you can bear to be despised, that is a great thing, more than all the other virtues.

194. An old man said, 'Anyone who bears humiliation, scorn, and punishment can be saved.'

195. An old man said, 'Do not be intimate with the abbot and do not visit him much, for you will learn a certain over-familiarity of speech from it and finally you will want to be superior in your turn.'

196. A holy man who had seen someone in the act of committing a sin wept bitterly and said, 'He today, and I tomorrow. In truth, even if some-

one commits sin in your presence, do not judge him, but consider yourself a worse sinner than he.'

197. In a monastery there was a brother who took upon himself all the brethrens' accusations. He even went so far as to accuse himself of fornication, saying he was guilty of it. Some of the brethren who were unaware of his practice began to murmur against him, saying, 'This person commits many sins and does not work', but the abba, who knew his practice, said to the Fathers, 'I would rather have the single mat he makes with humility than all these you make with pride. Do you wish for proof of this from God?'—and he had all the mats made by the brethren brought, and the single mat made by the brother. He lit a fire and threw them onto it. All the mats burnt except the brother's. Seeing this, the brethren were filled with fear, and prostrated themselves; and henceforth they considered him as a father.

198. A monk received a blow from someone, and he accepted the blow and bowed in penitence before the one who hit him.

199. An old man said, 'Pray God to give you compunction of heart and humility. Pay continual attention to your sins, and do not judge others, but consider yourself inferior to all. Do not be friendly with a woman, a boy, or a heretic; and restrain yourself from too great freedom of speech. Control your tongue and your belly and do not touch wine. If someone speaks to you about something do not argue with him but say, 'Yes'; and if he speaks ill say to him, 'You know what you are saying', but do not argue with him about the way he speaks. This is what humility is.'

200. An old man said, 'You must not say in your heart against your brother that you are more vigilant or more ascetic than he is, but by the grace of Christ submit yourself in a spirit of poverty and sincere charity so that you may not lose your labour through the spirit of vainglory. Indeed, it is written, "Let him who thinks he is standing take heed lest he fall".' (1 Cor. 10:12.)

201. Someone asked an old man, 'How is it that some say, "We see visions of angels"?'—and he replied, 'Happy is he who always sees his sins'.

202. There was an old man on the banks of the Jordan who went into a cave during the hot weather. Inside he found a lion who began to bare his teeth and roar. The old man said to him, 'Why get annoyed? There is enough room here for you and me, and if you do not like it, then go away.' Not able to stand it, the lion went away.

203. A brother questioned an old man saying, 'Why is it that when I bow in penitence to someone who has something against me I do not see that his thought towards me is purified?' The old man said to him, 'Tell me the truth, do you not justify yourself in your heart, saying you are making him an act of penitence though actually it is he who has wronged you—and you are asking his pardon in order to obey the commandment?' The brother said, 'Yes, that is so.' Then the old man said to him, 'This is the reason why God does not move him to make his peace with you, for you do not do penance with conviction, as having sinned against him, but you consider him as having sinned against you. Now, even if he has sinned against you, you must convince yourself in your heart that it is you who have sinned against him, and you must vindicate your brother; then God will persuade him to make his peace with you.' The old man told him of the following instance:

'There were some devout lay people who went all together to become monks. Carried away by zeal which was not according to the words of the Gospel, but without knowing this, they castrated themselves for the Kingdom of Heaven's sake. When he heard of it, the Archbishop turned them out. Considering they had done rightly, they rose up against him, saying, "We have castrated ourselves for the Kingdom of Heaven's sake, and he has turned us out. Let us go and see the Archbishop of Jerusalem", and they went to tell him everything. The Archbishop said to them, "I also shall drive you away." Saddened by this, they went to Antioch to the Archbishop and told him about themselves, and in his turn the Archbishop sent them away. They said to one another, "Let us go to Rome to see the Pope, and he will do justice to us before all the others." So they went to the Archbishop of Rome and told him what all the Archbishops had done to them. "We have come to you because you are the head of all of them." But in his turn he said to them, "I too am driving you away, and you are excommunicated." Not knowing what else to do, they said one to another, "They all say the same thing because they meet together at the synods. Well, then, let us go to that Saint of God, Epiphanius, Bishop of Cyprus

He is a prophet and not a respecter of persons." As they were drawing near the city, Epiphanius had a revelation about them, and he sent someone to meet them and tell them not to enter the city. Then, coming to their senses, they said to one another, "Indeed, we have sinned. Even if those others drove us away unjustly, it cannot be so with this prophet. It is because God has revealed something concerning us to him." So they accused themselves sincerely of what they had done. Then God, who knows hearts, seeing that they had truly repented, influenced the Bishop of Cyprus, Epiphanius, who sent in search of them, and after an exhortation he received them into communion and wrote to the Archbishop of Alexandria, "Receive your children, for in truth they have repented".'

Then the old man said, 'That is the healing of a man, and that is what God looks for: casting one's sin before oneself in the presence of God.'

OF LONG-SUFFERING

204. A monk who was given to hard work saw someone who was carrying a dead man on a bier and he said to him, 'Do you carry the dead? Go and carry the living.'

205. They said of a monk that the more someone despised or vexed him, the more he ran towards him, saying, 'Such men are a cause of progress for zealous people, while those who praise deceive and trouble the soul. Indeed, it is written, "Those who call you blessed are deceiving you."'

206. Some thieves came one day to the dwelling of an old man and said to him, 'We have come to take everything that is in your cell.' He said to them, 'My children, take what seems good to you.' So they took what they found in the cell and went away. Now they forgot a purse which happened to be hanging there. The old man picked it up and ran after them, calling out, 'Take this which you have forgotten from the cell.' Filled with wonder at the old man's long-suffering, they put back everything in its place in the cell and did penance, saying one to another, 'Truly this is a man of God'.

207. Some brothers came to visit a holy old man who dwelt in a desert place. Outside his dwelling they found some children pasturing animals, and they were uttering indecent words. After the brothers had manifested their thoughts to him and been helped by his wisdom, they said to the old man, 'Abba, how can you bear these children, and why do you not tell them not to cry out like this?' The old man said to them, 'Indeed, brothers, there are days when I want to give them such an order, but then I reproach myself, saying to myself, "If I am not able to bear this small inconvenience, how would I bear a great temptation if it fell upon me?" That is why I say nothing to them, to accustom myself to bear whatever comes.'

208. It was said of a brother who was neighbour to a great old man that when he went to his cell he robbed him. Now the old man saw it and did not reproach him but worked all the harder, saying, 'No doubt the brother needs it'. Now the old man was seriously inconvenienced and scarcely able to provide himself with bread. When he was at the point of death, the brothers were standing round him, and seeing the one who robbed him, he said, 'Come here', and he kissed his hands and said, 'I give thanks for these hands, for it is because of them that I am going to the kingdom of heaven.' The brother was filled with compunction and repented, and he became a tried monk because of what he had seen done by the great old man.

209. One of the old men told how he had heard it said by some saints that there are young ones who lead the old to life, and he related what follows: 'There was an old man, a drunkard, who used to make a mat every day and sell it in the village and drink the price. Later a brother came to dwell with him and he also made a mat. The old man took that as well, sold it, and drank the price of the two mats, only bringing a little bread back to the brother in the evening. He did this for three years without the brother saying anything. After that time the brother said to himself, "Look how deprived I am, I eat scarcely any bread; I will get up and go away from here." Then he pondered within himself, saying, "Where should I go? I will, rather, stay here, for it is for God's sake that I live the common life." Immediately an angel appeared to him and said, "Do not go away, for tomorrow I am coming for you." The same day the brother begged the old man, saying, "Do not go away, for my friends are going to

fetch me today." When the time came for the old man to go out, he said to the brother, "They will not come today, my child, they have been delayed." But the brother said, "Yes, abba, they will certainly come", and while he was speaking to him, he fell asleep. Then the old man said, weeping, "Woe is me, my child, because I have lived negligently for many years, and in a short time you have saved your soul by your endurance." From that day, the old man grew wise and became a tried monk.'

210. The old men used to tell of another man who had a boy who lived with him. He saw him doing something which he ought not and said to him once, 'Do not do that', but the other did not listen. As he disobeyed him, the old man took no further notice of him and left him to his own judgment. The young man shut the door of the cell where the provisions were kept and left the old man fasting for thirteen days. The latter did not ask where he was or where he had gone. Now the old man had a neighbour who, when he realized that the brother was late, made a little food and offered it to him, inviting him to eat. But when he asked, 'Why is the brother late?' the old man said, 'He will come back when he can.'

211. It was said that some philosophers came one day to test the monks. Now one of the monks passed by clothed in beautiful garments, and the philosophers said to him, 'Come here', but he, in anger, scorned them. Another monk, a Libyan, passed by, and they said to him, 'You old scoundrel of a monk, come here', and they compelled him to come. They gave him a box on the ear, but he offered them the other cheek. At once the philosophers arose and prostrated themselves before him, saying, 'Truly this is a monk'. Then they sat him down in their midst and questioned him, 'What do you, in the desert, do more than we? You fast, and we also fast; you watch, and we also watch; and all you do, we do also. What more do you who live in the desert do?' The old man said to them, 'We hope in the grace of God and we guard our thoughts.' They said to him, 'We are not able to do that.' Edified, they took their leave.

212. There were two monks living in one place, and a great old man came to visit them with the intention of testing them. He took a stick and began to bang about the vegetables of one of them. Seeing it, the brother hid himself, and when only one shoot was left, he said to the old man,

57

'Abba, if you will, leave it so that I can cook it that we may eat together.'
Then the old man bowed in penitence to the brother, saying, 'Because of
your long-suffering, the Holy Spirit rests on you, brother.'

OF CHARITY

213. An old man sent his disciple to Egypt to bring back a camel so as
to be able to take his baskets to Egypt. When the brother brought the
camel to Scetis he met another old man who said to him, 'If I had known
you were going to Egypt, I would have asked you to bring back a camel
for me also.' The brother went and told his father this, and he said to him,
'Take the camel and give it to him saying, "As for us, we are not ready for
it yet, so take it". Go to Egypt with him and bring back the camel so that
we can transport our produce also.' So the brother went to see the old
man and said to him, 'My abba says we are not ready yet; take it and use it
as you need to.' So the old man took the camel and loaded it with his
baskets. When they arrived in Egypt and had unloaded the baskets, the
brother took the camel and said to the old man, 'Pray for me'. The other
said to him, 'Where are you going?' The brother said, 'To Scetis, so that I
can collect our baskets also.' Filled with compunction, the old man bowed
in penitence, weeping and saying, 'Forgive me, for your great charity has
robbed me of my reward.'

214. An old man said, 'When someone asks something of you, even if
you do violence to yourself in giving it to him, your thought must take
pleasure in the gift according to that which is written, "If someone asks
you to go a mile, go two miles with him". That is to say, if someone asks
something of you, give it to him with your whole soul and spirit.'

215. There were two brothers at the Cells. The elder said to the
younger, 'Brother, let us dwell together.' He said to him, 'I am a sinner, I
cannot live with you, abba', but the other insisted on it, saying, 'Yes, we
can do it'. Now the old man was pure and did not like hearing from a
monk that he had thoughts of fornication. The younger brother said to
him, 'Leave me for a week and we will speak of it again.' When the week
was over the old man came, and the younger, wishing to test him, said to
him, 'I have fallen into great temptation, abba, this week. Indeed, when I

went to the village on an errand I sinned with a woman.' The old man said to him, 'Do you repent?' The brother answered, 'Yes.' The old man said, 'I will bear the half of your sin with you.' Then the brother said to him, 'Henceforth we can be together', and they dwelt the one with the other until they died.

216. It was said of a brother that having made some baskets he was putting on the handles when he heard his neighbour saying, 'What can I do? Market day is near and I have no handles to put on my baskets.' Then he took the handles off his own baskets and brought them to the brother, saying, 'Here are these handles which I have over; take them and put them on your baskets.' So he caused his brother's work to succeed by neglecting his own.

217. They told of an old man at Scetis who, when he was ill, longed for some fresh bread. When he heard of it, one of the brothers who was an athlete picked up his sheepskin, put some dry loaves into it, and went off to Egypt to exchange them, and he brought them back to the old man. When they saw that they were still warm, they were astonished. The old man refused to eat them, saying, 'It is my brother's blood', but the old men persuaded him to eat them, saying, 'For the Lord's sake, eat, so that the brother's sacrifice be not in vain', and at this he ate.

218. A brother asked an old man, 'How is it that in these days some afflict themselves in their manner of life and do not receive grace as the ancients did?' The old man said to him, 'In those days there was charity and each one caused his neighbour to make progress, but now that charity has grown cold, each one pulls his neighbour back, and that is why we do not receive grace.'

219. Three brothers went harvesting one day and agreed to harvest together, but on the first day one of them fell ill and returned to his cell. One of the two who remained said to his companion, 'Brother, you see that our brother is ill; make an extra effort, and I will do the same, and I am sure that helped by his prayers we shall be able to harvest his share.' When the work was finished and they came to receive their wages, they called the brother and said to him, 'Come and take your wage, brother.' He said, 'What wage should I receive, since I have not harvested?' They

said, 'Thanks to your prayers the harvest is done, so come and receive your wages.' They argued about it for a long time amongst themselves, the first saying he ought to receive nothing, the others refusing to go away if he did not take it. So they went to see a great old man, for him to judge the case. The brother said to him, 'Father, we three went harvesting. While we were going to the fields the first day, I fell ill and returned to my cell without having harvested a single day, and the brethren are compelling me, saying, "Come and accept the wage for the harvesting you have not done"', but the two others said, 'Father, we three received work to do, and if we had been three we should not have been able to do all the work, but thanks to the brother's prayers, we were able to finish the harvest quickly, and we said to him, "Take your wage", and he refuses to do so.' Hearing this, the old man was filled with wonder, and he said to his disciple, 'Give the signal for all the brethren to assemble.' When they were all there he said to them, 'Come, my brothers, and hear just judgment today.' Then the old man told them the whole story, and they judged that the brother should receive his wage and do with it whatever seemed right to him.' Then the brother went away weeping with sorrow.

220. An old man said, 'Our fathers were accustomed to send young brothers who wanted to live in solitary asceticism back to the cells and to watch over them for fear that, being tempted by the devil, one of them should suffer harm through his ideas. If by chance one of them happened to be ill, they brought him to the church. A basin of water was brought and prayer was made over the sick man, and all the brethren washed him, throwing water over him, and he was healed at once.'

221. Two old men had lived together for many years and had never fought with one another. The first said to the other, 'Let us also have a fight like other men do.' The other replied, 'I do not know how to fight.' The first said to him, 'Look, I will put a brick between us, and I will say it is mine, and you say, "No, it is mine", and so the fight will begin.' So they put a brick between them and the first said, 'This brick is mine', and the other said, 'No, it is mine', and the first responded, 'If it is yours, take it and go'—so they gave it up without being able to find an occasion for argument.

222. An old man said, 'Never have I wished to do something useful for myself which would harm my brother, for I have the firm hope that my brother's gain is a work full of fruit for me.'

223. An ascetic, having found someone possessed by the devil and unable to fast, and being (as it is written) moved by the love of God, and seeking not his own good but the good of the other, prayed that the devil might pass into himself and that the other might be liberated. God heard his prayer. The ascetic, overwhelmed by the devil, gave himself with re-doubled insistence to fasting, prayer, and *ascesis*. At last, because of his charity, God drove the devil away from him after a few days.

224. A brother questioned an old man, saying, 'Here are two brothers. One of them leads a solitary life for six days a week, giving himself much pain, and the other serves the sick. Whose work does God accept with the greater favour?' The old man said, 'Even if the one who withdraws for six days were to hang himself up by his nostrils, he could not equal the one who serves the sick.'

225. A brother served one of the Fathers who was ill. His body had suppurating wounds which exuded a bad smell. The brother's thoughts suggested to him, 'Flee, for you cannot bear the intensity of this bad smell.' But the brother took a vessel and put that which came from the sick man's sores into it. When his thoughts began to tell him to flee, he said to them, 'Do not flee, do not drink this putrefying stuff'. So the brother suffered and went on serving the old man, and seeing the brother's labour, God healed the old man.

226. Some brothers at Scetis were sitting cleaning rope, and one of them whose *ascesis* had made him ill began to cough and to spit. Though he did not wish to do so, he spluttered over a brother who was tormented by the thought of saying to the sick man, 'Stop spitting over me'. Fighting against his thoughts, he said to himself, 'If you are ready to eat the spittle, speak.' Then he said to himself, 'Do not eat it, and say nothing to him.'

227. One of the Fathers went off to the city to sell his manual work, and seeing a naked beggar he was moved by compassion and gave him his

own habit. The poor man went and sold it. When he heard what he had done, the old man was very annoyed and repented of having given him the habit. That night Christ appeared to the old man in a dream; he was wearing the habit and said to him, 'Do not grieve, for see I am wearing that which you have given me.'

ABOUT THE FATHERS WHO HAD THE GIFT OF VISION

228. One of the Fathers used to say that some old men were sitting one day and talking of what was useful to the soul. One of them had the gift of vision, and he saw angels who were waving branches in honour of the old men, but when one of them began to speak of irrelevant things the angels withdrew, and some pigs walked amongst the old men bringing a bad smell and messing up everything. As soon as they began once again to speak of what was useful to the soul, the angels returned to do them honour.

229. An old man said, 'This is what that saying of Scripture means, "I will turn away from two sins of Tyre, and even from three, but I will not turn away from four" (Amos 1:9). The three sins are: thinking evil, consenting to it, and saying so; but the fourth is actually doing the evil. From this the anger of God is not turned away.'

230. It was said of a great old man at Scetis that when the brethren were building a cell they went joyfully to lay the foundations and did not stop till it was finished. As he went one day to the cell that was being built, he was very grave. The brethren said to him, 'Why are you grave and sad, abba?' He said to them, 'This place is going to be deserted, my children. Indeed, I have seen a great fire in Scetis and the brothers putting it out with branches. It flared up again, and once more they put it out. A third time it flared up and spread throughout Scetis and none could stop it any more. That is why I am grave and sad.'

231. An old man said, 'It is written, "The righteous shall flourish like a palm tree" (Ps. 92:12). This saying means that what proceeds from their lofty deeds is good and right and pleasant. The palm tree has a single heart, which is white, containing all that is good. One meets the same thing

amongst the righteous: their heart is simple, seeing only God; it is white, having the illumination which proceeds from faith; and all the work of the righteous is in their hearts. Like the palm tree, their sharp points are in order to defend themselves against the devil.'

232. An old man said, 'The Shunammite received Elias because she had no relations with a man (2 Kings 4:14). Now it is said that the Shunammite represents the soul and Elias the Holy Spirit. Likewise, when the soul withdraws from bodily cares, the Holy Spirit comes upon her and then, since she is barren, she is able to conceive.'

233. One of the Fathers said, 'The eyes of pigs have a natural conformation which makes them turn towards the ground and they can never look up to heaven, so is the soul of one who lets himself be carried away by pleasure. Once the soul is allowed to slip into the slough of enjoyment, she can no longer get out again.'

234. A great old man had become clairvoyant, and he affirmed with great vigour, 'The power that I have seen at the moment of baptism, I have also seen at the clothing of a monk when the habit is put on him.'

235. An old man one day received the grace of being able to see what passed, and he said, 'I have seen a brother meditating in his cell and the demons standing outside the cell. While the brother was meditating they were not able to enter, but when he stopped meditating, then the demons entered the cell and strove with him.'

236. One of the Fathers said that he had two brothers as neighbours, one of whom was a foreigner and the other a native. Now the foreigner was somewhat careless, but the native brother was very fervent. It came to pass that the foreigner died, and the old man (who was clairvoyant) saw a host of angels accompanying his soul. When he got to heaven and was on the point of entering there was an enquiry concerning him, and a voice came from on high which said, 'It is clear that he was somewhat careless, but for the sake of his pilgrimage, let him come in'. Later on, the native brother died, and all his relations came. The old man saw no angel anywhere then, and he was astonished and prostrated himself before God, saying, 'How did that foreigner who was careless receive such glory while

this one, who was fervent, has received nothing at all?' A voice came which said to him, 'This fervent monk, when he came to die, opened his eyes and saw his relations weeping and his soul was comforted; but the foreigner, even though he was careless, yet saw none of his own family and wept in affliction because of it; therefore God has consoled him.'

237. One of the Fathers related that there was an anchorite in the desert of Nicopolis whom a devout layman used to serve. There was also in the city a rich and godless man. Now it came to pass that the latter died and the whole city made a procession for him, including the bishop, with lights and incense. The anchorite's servant, according to his custom, went to take bread to the anchorite, and he found he had been eaten by a hyena. He fell face downwards on the ground, saying, 'Lord, I shall not rise till you have explained the meaning of all this to me. That godless man received great pomp, and the monk who served you night and day has died like this.' Then an angel of the Lord came to say to him, 'That godless man did a little good, and he has found his reward here below so as not to receive any remission above; but this anchorite, although he was adorned with all the virtues, yet had some faults as a man. He has paid for them here below so as to be found pure before God.' Satisfied, the servant went away, giving glory to God for his judgments, for they are true.

238. It was said that an old man prayed God that he might see the demons, and it was revealed to him, 'You have no need to see them,' but the old man persisted, saying, 'Lord, you are able to protect me with your hand'. So God opened his eyes and he saw the demons like bees around a man, grinding their teeth against him, and the angels of the Lord drove them away.

The End

CHRONOLOGICAL TABLE OF EGYPTIAN MONASTICISM

249–51   Persecution by the Emperor Decius.

c. 251   Antony the Great born.

c. 292   Pachomius born.

300   Peter, Bishop of Alexandria.

303   Edict of Persecution.

311   Martyrdom of Peter of Alexandria.

c. 320   Pachomius founds community at Tabennesi.

324   Constantine sole emperor.

325   Council of Nicea. Alexandria established as second in ecclesiastical importance only to Rome.

328   Athanasius, Archbishop of Alexandria.

330   Amoun in Nitria.
        Macarius the Egyptian in Scetis.

337   Death of Constantine, as a Christian.

340   Foundation of the Cells from Nitria.

346   Death of Pachomius.

356   Death of Antony the Great.

357   Athanasius writes *Life of Antony.*

370   Basil, Bishop of Caesarea. Writes *Rules.*

373   Death of Athanasius.

373–75   Rufinus and Melania visit Egypt.

379   Death of Basil.

381   Council of Constantinople.

389   Death of Gregory of Nazianzus.

399–400   Origenist controversy splits Egyptian monasticism.

407–08   First devastation of Scetis by Barbarians.

c. 412   Rufinus' *History of the Monks in Egypt* is completed; he dies. Cyril, Archbishop of Alexandria.

419–20   Palladius writes *Lausiac History.*

431   Council of Ephesus.

434   Second devastation of Scetis.

444   Death of Cyril of Alexandria.

451   Council of Chalcedon.

455   Sack of Rome by the Vandals.
        (*Apophthegmata* are written down and collected during the fifth century. Process of copying, editing, amplifying begins.)

SUGGESTIONS FOR FURTHER READING

Background

Peter Brown, *The World of Late Antiquity*, London, 1971.

Owen Chadwick, *John Cassian*, CUP, 1950.

Derwas Chitty, *The Desert a City*, Oxford, 1966; reprinted Crestwood, New Jersey, 1978.

E. R. Hardy, *Christian Egypt*, New York, 1952.

Translations of some Early Sources

Pachomian Koinonia, trans. Armand Veilleux, Cistercian Publications, 3 vols., 1982.

The Letters of St Antony the Great, trans. Derwas Chitty, SLG Press, 1975.

The Letters of Ammonas, trans. Derwas Chitty, SLG Press, 1979.

Life of St Antony by Athanasius, trans. R. T. Meyer, Ancient Christian Writers, vol. 10, Washington 1950.

The Ascetic Works of St Basil, trans. W. K. Lowther Clarke, SPCK, 1925.

Three Byzantine Saints, trans. Dawes and Baynes, Blackwells, 1948. (This is a translation of the Lives of Daniel the Stylite, Theodore of Studion, and John the Almsgiver.)

Evagrius Ponticus, *Praktikos and Chapters on Prayer*, trans. John Eudes Bamberger, Cistercian Publications, USA, 1970.

The Ladder of Divine Ascent, John Climacus, trans. Colm Luibheid and Norman Russell with an Introduction by Kallistos Ware, Classics of Western Spirituality, SPCK, London 1982.

Palladius, *The Lausiac History*, trans. R. T. Meyer, Ancient Christian Writers, vol. 34, Washington, 1965.

Lives of the Desert Fathers, trans. Benedicta Ward and Norman Russell, Mowbrays, 1981.

Other Selections of *Apophthegmata* in English

Wallis Budge, *The Wit and Wisdom of the Christian Fathers of Egypt*, Oxford, 1934.

Owen Chadwick, *Western Asceticism*, SCM Press, 1958.

Thomas Merton, *The Wisdom of the Desert*, Sheldon Press, 1973.

Helen Waddell, *The Desert Fathers*, Constable and Co., 1936.

Benedicta Ward, *Sayings of the Desert Fathers*, Mowbrays, 1979.

FAIRACRES PUBLICATIONS

Complete List

All titles listed above are obtainable—postage extra—from SLG Press, Convent of the Incarnation, Fairacres, Oxford OX4 1TB, England.

* For sale in UK only

† Not for sale in USA

Price list March 1986